JOHANNES OCKEGHEM

JOHANNES OCKEGHEM AND HIS CHOIR

Johannes Ockeghem

BY ERNST KRENEK

Great Religious Composers

Edited by John J. Becker

SHEED & WARD · NEW YORK · 1953

FOREWORD

THIS book on Johannes Okeghem by Ernst Krenek is the first of a series of small books called "Great Religious Composers," through which we hope to interest the general public as well as those persons responsible for church music, in the rich treasures of the past so that this music and these composers may again become a part of the living present. That these composers were vital personalities in their day is an historical record but the present-day public knows little about them and is almost completely unfamiliar with their names.

With a few exceptions the religious music of the early masters has practically fallen into oblivion. Church music as a whole is now decadent, and instead of the sublime music of the earlier centuries, we have substituted sentimental and romantic music that has little to do with religious aspirations and is in no way compatible with Christian ideas of art.

These books will not be technical and the chief emphasis will be on an evaluation of the men and their music. The composers will be discussed in the light of their own times and also in relation to the twentieth-century composers and any influence they may have had on them, for strange as it may seem, it is the present-day composer who is reviving an interest in these men and their great music.

Each book will be written by an important musical personality and will include a bibliography, a list of published works that are available, and a list of any recordings that have been made.

JOHN J. BECKER, B.M., Mus.D.
Editor
Composer in Residence and
Professor of Music
Barat College of the Sacred Heart
Lake Forest, Illinois

ERNST KRENEK

ERNST KRENEK was born August 23, 1900 in Vienna. He attended the Academy of Music in Vienna, and the Academy of Music in Berlin, and studied at the University of Vienna where he specialized in Philosophy and the History of Art and Music. He came to America in 1937 and has been a citizen of the United States since 1945.

From 1939 to 1947, he carried on extensive research in the melodic design of Gregorian Chant, in the cantus firmus technique and the modal theory of the Middle Ages, in an attempt to work out for himself some theoretical foundation of the twelve-tone technique of which he is a master, and one of the leading exponents.

During that period he wrote religious choral works, the most important being the "Lamentatio Jeremiae Prophetae," and operas with religious backgrounds, namely, "Carl V" and "Tarquin."

Mr. Krenek's orchestral works have been performed by the major orchestras both here and abroad, and his operas have been staged in the most important opera houses in Europe.

Mr. Krenek is now residing in Los Angeles.

JOHANNES OCKEGHEM

Hidden Treasures

As I recall the old days when I was a boy in Vienna, and we went, off and on, to High Mass at the ancient cathedral of St. Stephen or the neo-Gothic Votivkirche where my piano teacher was organist, my memory of the musical treat to which we were looking forward is always associated with the little chirping sounds typical of an orchestra tuning up. It was not the cheerful, uninhibited gurgling and squeaking noises that would come from the pit of an operatic orchestra; it was discreet, subdued, timid, as would befit the dignified atmosphere of the sanctuary: a few violinists quickly plucking a string or two to test the pitch once more, an oboe player softly trying a couple of notes to make sure of the condition of his reed—and as soon as the celebrant had made his entrance there would pour forth solemn or gay blasts of brass, the woodwinds would add a layer of silvery threads, and the strings would sing out in soaring melodies. Soon the chorus would join them, and when the sacred text turned to the contrition of the "Miserere nobis" or to the mysticism of "Et incarnatus est," we would hear the soloists indulge in long-drawn-out emotional phrases, or even in some exacting coloraturas. Usually the final sections of the "Gloria" and the "Credo" blossomed out in elaborate, majestic, and eventually briskly animated fugues, the great waves of sound reverberating thunderously from the high pillars and through the vaulted naves of the huge cathedral. In our suburban parish church the musical part of the service was usually on a more modest scale, but even there they would occasionally try their hands at the orchestral masses by Haydn, Mozart, Beethoven, or Schubert, which to every Austrian represent the acme of ecclesiastical music.

The Baroque Mass marks the final participation of the Roman Church to this day in the greatness of music. In our time even this offering is welcome only in and around the countries of its origin, for in many parts of the Catholic world ecclesiastical authorities and church congregations find the Baroque mass too worldly, too operatic, to be used for regular church services. It is not easy to understand how many of the later contributions to church music—for the most part lachrymose, sentimental, and artistically second-hand and second-rate material—could be judged less worldly, and more suited for the religious purpose, but this is a question which we shall not discuss on these pages. The fact remains that anyone attending religious services at an average church would hardly be able to guess that any music of true artistic significance had originated under the inspiration of the Church, and of what she stands for.

This is not only sad but also strange, for there was a time during which all music that aspired to the epithet "great"— and in many cases it deserved it—was written in the service of the Church. This was not a short period by any means, it lasted nearly a thousand years. There are many factors which might explain why those in charge of church music make no use of that music, with the exception of a few works of only one of the latest composers of that great era: Palestrina. Even those are heard rather sporadically. The main reason for this neglect, one which sums up all other explanations, is that this music is practically unknown to anybody except the scholars who have made it their business to explore it from an historical viewpoint.

Music is the only art in Western civilization which is familiar to the public at large solely through its accomplishments during the past two hundred and fifty years. The average consumer of music will hardly be aware of the fact that our music, though admittedly a very young art, has a traceable recorded history of over thirteen hundred years. A person interested in literature may easily enjoy the full continuity of man's literary efforts from Homer to Hemingway. A similar panorama of the pictorial arts will be somewhat more limited in regard to the time span that it may take in, but it is still quite possible to acquire some familiarity with mediaeval painting, as nowadays even small provincial museums own at least a few specimens of that art—not to speak of countless excellent reproductions. And even the art lover who is not able to travel to the old world to inspect the innumerable monuments of ancient architecture can inform himself on it from descriptions and pictures. Only the friend of music is out of luck, for in concerts, over the radio, and wherever else music is made audible to him, he will hardly ever hear anything older than Bach or Handel, which is early eighteenth century. Purcell, Monteverdi, Schütz, of seventeenth-century fame, will appear once in a great while on some very special occasions. Behind Palestrina, of whose thousands of compositions only three or four are known to the initiated, a few names emerge from the darkness like ghosts, for no note of music is associated with them.

Of course the music lover is not to be blamed for his ignorance. In comparison to the other arts, music is at a serious disadvantage since it needs performance in order to come into its own. A painting can be looked at the minute the painter has applied the last stroke of his brush. A book can be read once the author has added the period to the last sentence and the printer has done his work. But up to relatively recent times it was not even possible to read the music of the Middle Ages. It was preserved in unique copies of the original manuscripts, oftentimes buried in remote

3

archives, hardly accessible to laymen and difficult to decipher even to the experts in ancient methods of notation. Nowadays an increasing number of editions in modern notation are available, but what good does it do to the man-in-the-street who is unable to read music? He is excluded from enjoying those musical treasures unless the music is being performed for him.

Although music is among the youngest of the arts in Western civilization, it has undergone most rapid and spectacular changes in its short time of existence. This condition is to some extent responsible for the fact that the wonderful accomplishments of the past fell so quickly into oblivion. The situation is paradoxical. While the general orientation of the present day's musical life is stubbornly geared to the past, to the extent of haughtily ignoring present production, the music of the farther distant past is equally excluded, although a better acquaintance with it would not only be rewarding in itself, but would also serve to open ears and minds to the message of the modern composer. There are many aspects of contemporary music which are more akin to concepts of the mediaeval mind than to those of the period immediately preceding our own. Thus, unveiling the features of ancient religious music will not only add to the glory of the Church, but also broaden the horizon and the receptive capacities of music lovers in general.

The Fifteenth Century

ONE of the most interesting, and not yet fully explored, periods in music is the fifteenth century. Although the thoughts of some of its great masters are now coming to light in beautiful and carefully edited collections of their complete works, we do not yet have a clear understanding of the musical significance of their contributions. It does not mean belittling the painstaking work of the musicologists who have devoted a staggering amount of labor to preparing those editions, when we state that their work has so far remained only a preliminary step toward a study of the amazing wealth of material from the vantage point of the artist. The musicologist is mainly interested in historical facts. He wishes to establish an authentic text by comparing and evaluating critically the various copies of a work that may be in existence. Beyond that he wants to place the author that has come under consideration as exactly as possible into the context of the historical evolution as the scholar sees it. He will try to trace all possible influences that may have acted upon the composer, as well as those that emanated from him upon his contemporaries and successors. All this is perhaps interesting and frequently necessary in order to obtain a complete picture of the material on hand. But it does not yet touch upon the unique artistic personality of the composer so examined, it does not explain the aesthetic and spiritual value of his accomplishments. Some outstanding musicologists have presented critical analyses of that kind concerning masters of later periods, but very little has been written so far about the great musical creators of the fifteenth century.

On the following pages we shall attempt to sketch a profile of Johannes Ockeghem. Since this paper is addressed to the general public, we have refrained from introducing and discussing examples of his music, for the benefit of those of our readers who are not able to read such examples. To the same extent as this omission makes the reading easier, it renders the writer's task more difficult, for to explain technicalities of music is no problem if the explanation can refer to the music itself and be verified with the aid of musical illustrations. Perhaps this imposed limitation is only for the

5

best, as it will check any temptation on our part to probe too deeply into the technical aspects of Ockeghem's music. The unavoidable minimum of technical matters which have to be touched upon will be dealt with in such a way that even the unprepared layman will understand what we are talking about.

The Strange Case of Johannes Ockeghem

THE case of Johannes Ockeghem offers much interesting material to the discussion of the ever intriguing question: What is greatness, what constitutes lasting value in music? Here is a composer whose name has remained in evidence ever since the fifteenth century, in which he lived and enjoyed high respect and great reputation. But nearly until our own time hardly anything else of him was in evidence. Only a very small part of his musical output was known in fragmentary excerpts that were carried as illustrations in learned books on the theory and history of music. Apart from their being fragments—that is, passages of music lifted out of their larger contexts—these examples were not edited for practical use, so that it was not even possible to test whether Ockeghem's music was still alive, whether or not it carried any significance as expression and communication for later generations, whether it had anything to say.

The experts—that is, those scholars whose writings are read by hardly anybody but other experts—kept on mentioning and, to some extent, discussing Ockeghem because they were convinced that he had contributed something important to the evolution of music. We know that the thought processes of the nineteenth century in all fields placed an extraordinary emphasis upon the concept of evolution. It is well known how this concept dominated natural science, and how it also engulfed the humanities, especially the writing of history, which was seen as an unbroken line of progress from humble, "primitive" beginnings to the proud achievements of the present. Applied to the history of music this concept once in a while leads to astounding results. Reading such older disquisitions, we frequently get the impression that history is seen as a sort of express train in motion, and that the individuals who have made this history are evaluated mainly in their quality as operators, as to how much or how little they have contributed to the speed and direction of the moving train. The criterion of judgment is, of course, the point at which the observer stands at the moment of his writing. There has never been the slightest doubt that history's one and only sense and purpose was to move as swiftly and directly toward that point, which, with as much superb self-assurance as disarming naiveté, was assumed to be the goal and supreme fulfillment of the creation.

Hardly ever has anybody caught in this kind of reasoning realized that the train of history has stopped once in a while, and its crew members perhaps accomplished things which were important and significant then and there, without reference to future consummations. After all, those poor fellows did not even know that all they were supposed to do was to prepare the way for Wagner, Chopin, or some other nineteenth-century giant.

In the light of such principles Ockeghem appeared to the scholars noteworthy because he had added something to the musical knowledge of his time. That certainly is a point important enough to establish the composer as a significant figure. For the greatness of an artist undoubtedly rests upon those individual characteristics that distinguish him from his average contemporaries. He may not have entered upon the unknown territory of a hitherto unexplored musical idiom, as Arnold Schoenberg did, nor opened up new horizons and perspectives in flashes of lightning, like Beethoven. He may have done no more than impart to the contemporary styles of writing new qualities of lucidity, tenderness, intensity, as Mozart did; or developed accepted procedure to an unheard-of pinnacle of perfection, like Palestrina. At any rate, the great composer, in order to be recognized as great, must have accomplished something new in some respect.

The "Pure Cerebralist"

T HE scholars who had agreed on Ockeghem's importance as an artist who had made a noteworthy contribution to music, at the same time created the main obstacle to Ockeghem's music becoming better known. For up to recent times they were unanimous in pointing out that his contribution was mainly theoretical. In Cecil Gray's *The History of Music* we read, for instance: ". . . Ockeghem is a pure cerebralist, almost exclusively preoccupied with intellectual problems, and the most typical example in music of the kind of artist who, in the hackneyed phrase for which there is no adequate substitute, goes out of his way to create difficulties for the pleasure of overcoming them. Expression was for him a secondary consideration, if indeed it existed for him at all. He seems to have had something of the mentality of Arnold Schoenberg to-day, the same ruthless disregard of merely sensuous beauty, the same unwearying and relentless pursuit of new technical means for their own sake. He is the school master, the drill sergeant of music."[1]

The Oxford History of Music uses almost the same word-

[1] (London, 1928), p. 62.

8

ing to characterize Ockeghem: ". . . difficulties invented to be overcome . . . unremitting pursuit of canon and its kindred devices . . ."[2]

Grove's *Dictionary of Music and Musicians* quotes the German musicologist, Kiesewetter, to the effect that Ockeghem, in comparison to his predecessors, was distinguished "by a greater facility in counterpoint and fertility in invention . . . indicative of thought and sketched out with manifest design, being also full of ingenious contrivances of an obbligato counterpoint, at that time just discovered, such as augmentation, diminution, inversion, imitation, together with canons and fugues of the most manifold description . . . intellectual treat for the highly educated musicians."

All this amounts to a perhaps intriguing, but not particularly engaging picture of an unusually clever, but somewhat freakish composer. We are not surprised to observe that in the nineteenth century, in which these opinions on Ockeghem were formed, nobody bothered about excavating his music from its dusty repositories in remote archives. The only values which that century, almost exclusively, would acknowledge in music were of an emotional nature. Intuition, inspiration were the catchwords that dominated the period, and critical analysis of music was prevailingly focussed upon the alleged emotional contents of the work. The fact that this attitude was tied up with an extremely pedantic insistence upon a singularly dry system of academic rules reveals the strange dialectics obtaining in the history of art. We shall discuss these conditions later on. This is not the place to argue the merits or shortcomings of nineteenth-century mental attitudes. Every age is entitled to form its own historical and aesthetic judgments according to its own structure and disposition of mind. Obviously an era which found itself fully expressed in the dramatic explosions of Beethoven's symphonic cosmos, the languid sentiment of

[2] Vol. II, p. 211.

9

Chopin's pianistic poetry, the red-hot propaganda of Wagner's *Weltanschauung*, and the sensuous appeal of Verdi's vocal display, had little use for a composer who indulged in intellectual intricacies and "difficulties created to be overcome."

What puzzles the modern observer who is able to study the great majority of Ockeghem's works available in our time, is the question how those earlier scholars arrived at their quite articulate opinions about the character of the Flemish master's music. They admit that very little of it was known to them. It is not now possible to ascertain whether they based their judgment upon those fragments mentioned earlier, which were occasionally published in theoretical and historical treatises, or whether they took the trouble to inspect unpublished manuscripts preserved in archives. If they were satisfied with consulting those meager excerpts, their opinion was certainly resting upon extremely incomplete evidence, for everybody knew that Ockeghem had written more than those few examples of counterpoint. If they had seen a great deal of his work, their verdict must be considered incomprehensible, as we shall see later. What, then, prompted them to classify Ockeghem as a "pure cerebralist"?

The Thirty-six-voice "Twittering"

IT IS, of course, not possible to probe into the background of statements of that kind. As far as we can make out, the classification of Ockeghem as a dry intellectualist is a result of what one might call historical propaganda, although the remark which seems to have started the whole thing was undoubtedly made without any malice aforethought. It appears that the great Swiss theorist and critic, Glareanus, commented upon Ockeghem in his famous book *Dodeka-chordon,* which was published in Basel, Switzerland, in 1547. This book became widely known and influential, since in it the learned and temperamental author paved the way for the theoretical understanding of the evolutionary proc-esses that led from the musical idiom of the Middle Ages to that of modern times. The *Dodekachordon* is a remarkable book not only because of the lively presentation of its stim-ulating ideas, but also because of its abundance of musical examples culled from the literature of the century preceding its appearance. Among extensive excerpts from many com-posers Glareanus also quotes a fragment from Ockeghem, about which he says a few complimentary words, and goes on to say: "It is an established fact that he [Ockeghem] has arranged a certain twittering for thirty-six voices, which, however, we have not seen. *At least* he was admirable in re-gard to invention and acuteness of mind." (Italics mine.)

The report on the "thirty-six-voice twittering" doubtless intrigued later readers of Glareanus. Although Ockeghem was not the only composer to combine so staggering a num-ber of melodic lines into one polyphonic fabric, it seemed clear that only a man with unusual interest and skill in con-trapuntal techniques would attempt such a tour de force. Since one or two more technically intricate pieces of Ocke-ghem's were known, people soon made up their minds to the effect that either he had not written anything except those "artifices," or his other works would be of the same sort. It is fair to assume that if Glareanus, in spite of his closeness in time to Ockeghem, was not able (or not willing?) to take a look at that notorious thirty-six-voice canon, later observers were in no better position. Even today this work is not easily accessible, as it has not been published separately, but only as a musical illustration to learned treatises. Ockeghem's is not the only case of a composer who has become famous through the wrong thing. It is futile to speculate whether he might have completely fallen into oblivion, if his name had not survived on account of that contrapuntal stunt, or whether his true stature would have emerged earlier if his multi-voiced canon had not earned him the label of a "pure cerebralist." At any rate, the time has come for revealing Ockeghem as a truly great composer of all-round significance, and as the originator of profound, deeply felt religious music of highest artistic caliber and dignity.

We confess that our interest in Ockeghem was aroused for just those reasons that stood in the way of his music's becoming better known. The objection of "cerebralism" is so frequently leveled at many types of contemporary music that a modern composer becomes very alert to that sort of criticism. When he notices that one of the venerable masters of the past is exposed to the same kind of attack, he feels a certain solidarity with his long-departed colleague and tries to find out how the distant friend has incurred the adverse label. For the modern composer is quite sure that he himself is unjustly accused of an overdose of intellectualism, and he is anxious to find support in the historical analogy. Thus we have studied Ockeghem's work closely, and soon became convinced that his classification as a "pure cerebralist" is entirely unfounded. As we had suspected all along, he was relegated to the limbo which houses the pedantic "drill sergeants" because of his virtuosity in handling contrapuntal techniques. But before analysing the true character of his much more inclusive achievements, let us have a brief glance at the man and his life.

Who Was Johannes Ockeghem?

THE glance will have to be very brief by necessity, for in general very little is known of the personal lives of even the great figures of those by-gone ages. There was then in existence nothing like a "Who's Who in Music," which assiduously lists some relevant and much irrelevant data on some important and a great many inconsequential characters, including such trivia as their favorite hobbies and relaxations. Those ages were not as history-conscious as the past two centuries have been, and therefore not intent upon preserving every scrap of evidence, on the assumption that later generations would be as curious about such things as were the collectors of the material. They also were not as personality-conscious as we are in our period, when the significance of a man is recognized only to the extent to which he is able to build up notoriety through the almighty machinery of relentless publicity. Only in the two centuries preceding Ockeghem's appearance on the scene had a few names of individual composers emerged from the anonymity that had shrouded the creative efforts of the early Middle Ages.

The first, and frequently the most obscure, fact in the lives of those great men is the date and place of their birth, for when they were born, no one knew that they would become great men, and thus no one bothered with recording their entering this valley of tears. Frequently our most comprehensive information comes from their tombstones, on which one may find an epigrammatic summary of their biography. Other evidence of their earthly pilgrimage may be sifted out from documents gathering dust in archives, bookkeeping accounts listing fees and salaries paid out by some cathedral chapter or princely chamber to one of the geniuses we are interested in. Frequently these are the only clues from which we may infer where they lived at a given time. What little they may have left in the shape of letters or other personal papers has long ago disappeared in the destructive current of time. Nobody wrote their biographies, nobody interviewed them for newspapers, there were no magazines to record their moves and to catch snapshots of their more or less interesting physiognomies. Considering the appalling carelessness with which records of all kinds were obviously handled, we may well wonder that any of the music of those ages has reached us at all.

From such scattered data on Ockeghem's later life, it has been calculated that he was born some time around 1430, probably in Termonde in East Flanders, a province of what is now Belgium. As a matter of fact there was not far from Termonde a village of the name of Ockeghem, which made some historians believe that the composer's family might have come from there. The name Ockeghem (pronounced approximately Ōkaykhem, if you can make the "kh" sound quite rough) is Flemish, which is the language now spoken in the northeastern part of Belgium and is the same as Dutch. According to the truly cosmopolitan character of European culture in those ages, a great man was not considered any particular nation's private property, and the names of such men were freely adapted to other languages. Thus the master's name appears in no less than thirty-nine different spellings, reaching from such outlandish distortions as "Hoquegan" or "Obghuen" to the completely Germanized version, "Ockenheim," which Glareanus uses. Since the composer spent most of his life in French territory, his first name, Jan or Johannes (John) is frequently quoted as Jean. It seems that he was a choirboy at the cathedral of Antwerp in 1443 and 1444—this we know through records of some disbursements made to a fellow of that name. From

1446 to 1448 he was in the service of Charles, Duke of Bourbon, at Moulins, presumably also as a singer. The Bourbons belonged to the most prominent grandees of the French realm and had recently made Moulins, an ancient small town in central France, the capital of their duchy, a step which must have entailed considerable building activity. So far Moulins had been known only as the seat of several mills, whence it had received its name. There is some evidence that Ockeghem studied with Guillaume Dufay in Cambrai in 1450, although other sources suggest that he was a pupil of Gille Binchois, a Flemish composer of renown. It is typical that even so important a fact can not be definitely verified.

Three years later we find him at the court of Charles VII, King of France, in Paris. Relatively early in his life he must have made for himself a substantial reputation, for in 1459 he was appointed treasurer of the Abbey of St. Martin in Tours, a position of honor that is said to have been much coveted because of the considerable emoluments attached to it. It seems that this post was rather magnificently endowed. Not only had the treasurer a beautifully appointed town house at his disposal, he also benefited from several rich estates in the surrounding country and from various tithes and taxes due to him. On Ascension Day the butchers' guild of Tours had to deliver to him a lamb adorned with flowers and a quarter of beef, which was just one of the tokens offered to the dignity of his office. When the King of France visited Tours, the treasurer of St. Martin's was in charge of the elaborate ceremonies connected with such an event. He also was responsible for an important repository of crown jewels and archives containing state papers of high significance. In short, he was expected to behave like one of the great dignitaries of the realm.

The city of Tours, on the banks of the Loire river, had been a Roman colony and was one of the oldest seats of

Christianity in the territory of Gaule. St. Martin was bishop of Tours in the fourth century, and the abbey which was named after him became an important center of religious life. Its sanctuary was elevated to the rank of a collegiate church, and after a period of affiliation with the famous monastery of Cluny it became directly subordinate to the Holy See in Rome. Eventually it had its own bishops.

Ockeghem is back in Paris in 1461—perhaps he did not permanently reside at Tours, although he had to have a special dispensation for being away from the seat of his office—and in 1465 he is mentioned as master of the chapel royal in Paris. He was now in the service of Louis XI, who had succeeded Charles VII in 1461. He visited Spain in 1469, and Flanders, his native land, in 1484. Apparently he retained his office and his handsome establishment at Tours, and may have retired there. For it is in Tours that he died in approximately 1495. It is remarkable that even this date of Ockeghem's life is not verifiable by tangible evidence, although he was not only recognized in the artistic world, but was also an important figure in the officialdom of his day. Until late in the nineteenth century some scholars assumed that he was born considerably before 1430 and lived till 1512 or so, because one of the eulogies published some time after his death seemed to suggest that he lived to be close to one hundred. Only later indirect evidence has narrowed down the span of Ockeghem's life to what we have accepted on these pages as being most probable. Perhaps we could have learned the exact data of his life from the monument that is said to have been erected to his memory in Tours. But that too has become a victim of time, and is no more.

A Panorama of Ockeghem's World

WHAT was the world like in which Johannes Ockeghem lived and worked? Those of us who still recollect the peaceful years before 1914 may, upon glancing through a history book, come to the conclusion that Western Europe in the fifteenth century must have been a very uncomfortable place to live in. We read about wars, strife, dissension, destruction, misery, and more wars. However, the men of that day may subjectively not have found their period particularly dreadful. People were accustomed to look upon wars as the occasional, inevitable, violent manifestations of the congenital wretchedness of human nature, a consequence of original sin. Furthermore, wars were long in duration because of the slowness of operations, but at the same time geographically very limited. They consisted in a few bloody engagements involving hardly more than what we nowadays call a regiment, and the warriors were mercenaries, that is, professionals who had voluntarily chosen the cruel trade. Undoubtedly there was at all times insecurity because of marauding and looting, but on the whole this may not have amounted to much more damage than what is nowadays due to gangsterism and crime waves. Compared to what earlier and later centuries (especially the seventeenth) had to go through, the fifteenth does not seem to have been too bad.

In the area in which Ockeghem spent most of his life the main feature of the period was the consolidation and growing strength of France as a unified European power. In the beginning of the century the French had been badly beaten by the English, who at the time of Ockeghem's birth stood firmly entrenched in northern and eastern France, and King

Charles VII's reputation was at its lowest when the enemy besieged Orleans. It is well known what turned the tables: in 1429 Joan of Arc appeared on the scene, and within twenty years the English were thrown back to Calais, which remained their only beachhead on the continent. Although destitute and impoverished by war, inner dissension and corruption, France improved considerably in its morale as a consequence of these victories.

The account with the British being settled, Louis XI continued on the road to France's unification by turning against Burgundy. This powerful duchy of not always well-defined and somewhat unstable delineation comprised much of the territory of southeastern France and most of the provinces on the left bank of the Rhine, including parts of the Low Countries, among these also Flanders, so that politically Ockeghem ought to be considered a Burgundian. In the thirteenth and fourteenth centuries Burgundy had been a cultural center of prime importance, the cradle of many proud achievements in architecture, music, and painting. The clever maneuvering of the king of France aroused both the English and the Swiss against Burgundy, and when the latter administered to the Burgundians a catastrophic defeat in which their duke lost his life, it spelled the end of Burgundy's sovereignty.

As shrewdly as Louis XI had acted in engineering this outcome, he seems to have operated ineptly in securing the loot. The greater part of Burgundy fell to the Hapsburgs, and this, in connection with their establishment in Spain a little later, gave European history an aspect quite different from what it might have been if Burgundy had been joined to France right away, rather than in the course of time, as it was. While Charles VII and especially Louis XI were autocratic rulers of the old feudal style, Charles VIII, who succeeded to the throne in 1483, displayed somewhat different ideas on government. As early as 1484 he called a meeting of the States-General, by which we must not understand anything like a modern, democratic parliament, but a sort of consultative assembly of aristocrats mainly concerned with tax problems—anyhow, it was a sign that the despotic forms of government were loosening up. This body met in Tours, the city which we regard as Ockeghem's headquarters. At the end of his life, which approximately coincided with that of our composer, Charles VIII allowed himself to become involved in the political affairs of Italy, and this entailed more sacrifices and further delay of the progress of France. The general impression is that Ockeghem's life was spent in a country whose conditions were improving on the whole while he lived there. This is not entirely irrelevant when we try to picture for ourselves the atmosphere in which the composer carried out his work.

On the world horizon two events of greatest magnitude fell into the span of Ockeghem's life: the capture by the Turks of Constantinople in 1452 and the discovery of the New World in 1492. The composer died too early to become even remotely aware of the implications of this latter feat, but he must have experienced the build-up of general vitality, the storing up of incredible energies, that made possible the sudden and utterly fantastic expansion of the world of Western man.

The fall of Constantinople caused deep concern in the Christian mind and overshadowed the triumphant mood in which Pope Nicolas V had ordained a year of jubilee in 1450. He was the first Pope to rule peacefully over a Church that had been torn and shaken to its foundations by the exile at Avignon and long periods of schism and quarreling between rival aspirants to the Holy See. But in spite of the menace from the East and the religious unrest in the West, which would soon break out in the various Protestant movements, Nicolas V as well as his successors to the end of the century—Calixtus III (a Borgia), Pius II (Aeneas Sylvius

Piccolomini, a poet of some merit), Paul II, Sixtus IV, and Innocent VIII—expended sustained efforts toward making Rome and the Vatican into that unique repository of artistic and cultural treasures which has remained one of the marvels of this world. Suffice it to mention that the Sistine Chapel was conceived and constructed under Sixtus IV. Although Ockeghem's religious works were undoubtedly written for immediate use in the churches of his country, the awareness of working for an organization whose heads were most actively interested in sponsoring and supporting contemporary art can not have failed to be an inspiring factor in the composer's life.

In artistic and intellectual achievements the period was somewhat less prolific than one might expect considering the great music which it brought forth. It seems that the flowering which the other arts had seen in the Middle Ages was largely a matter of the past, while the new upsurge of creative power that was tied up with the concept of the Renaissance had not yet become manifest. Among Ockeghem's compatriots the painters Jan van Eyck, Roger van der Weyden, and Hugo van der Goes must be mentioned. The first named is credited with the invention of oil painting. The most important of Ockeghem's younger contemporaries among the painters was Hieronymus van Bosch, whose visions of hell are strangely akin to Ockeghem's music in their startling imagination and intricacy of detail. There is in these paintings a strong and somewhat anachronistic mediaeval flavor which, as we shall see, also characterizes Ockeghem's musical landscape.

When we look at the arts from the angle of music, architecture deserves our special attention, since much of its method in dealing with matter and space is analogous to the procedures of music in organizing sound and time. We shall take up this point again, when we discuss Ockeghem's work in more detail. The fifteenth century saw the development of the last phase of the Gothic style, usually called "flamboyant." This term refers to the rich and lavish detail of the ornamentation, in which flamelike curvatures play an important part. This newly gained ornamental exuberance contrasts somewhat with the relative simplicity of the over-all structures, which in turn had been more complex in earlier phases of the style. Ockeghem's native country produced some remarkable specimens of flamboyant Gothic in the town halls of Brussels, Louvain, and other places. The choir-boy may also have been impressed with the cathedral of Antwerp and its seven aisles, which had been under construction since 1354 and was completed in 1474.

The literary output of the century seems to be singularly limited. The French hobo poet, François Villon, stands out as a picturesque character, but he would hardly attract as much attention as he does, had he not been on the stage nearly alone.

Scholasticism, the dominant philosophy of the Middle Ages, was on its way out as a living expression of the thought processes of the era. The Renaissance mind turned away from Aristotle and began to derive its ideas from Plato. In Italy we come across the names of thinkers like Pico de Mirandola and Nicholas of Cusa.

However, the new spirit of the Renaissance, the full impact of "modern" times as expressed by Michelangelo or Raphael, who were born when Ockeghem was past middle age, made its appearance only later, after his death.

Gregorian Chant and "Ars Nova"

IF IT is then correct to say that the fifteenth century saw the greatest accomplishments in music, what was the status of music when Ockeghem entered the scene? The conventional textbooks on the history of music discuss the so-called three Netherland schools of composition and list Ockeghem as the leader of the second of these schools. Such classifications are typical of the simplification to which the average schoolmaster is prone to subject the historical evidence in order to hand it out to his charges in easily digestible portions.

Human life, which after all furnishes the subject matter for the bookkeepers of history, rarely develops in such neatly articulated phases, but is a continuous stream which gradually and subtly changes the face of the landscape through which it flows by countless slight movements, the significance of which is only dimly perceptible to those who cause them. Surely Ockeghem did not know that he was the head of the second Netherland school; no more was Guillaume Dufay aware of being the leader of the first.

In order to understand what went on, we have to cast just a glance at the evolution of the fourteenth century. There we encounter a phenomenon that had hardly ever occurred earlier in music history, although after the Renaissance it became a dominant factor. In the fourteenth century a musical movement started which was called by one of its spokesmen—Philippe de Vitry—the *Ars Nova*, the "new art." Never before had anybody thought of setting up a contemporary system of artistic principles against those of the past.

One might well say that this is the beginning of modernism in music. Of course we must not think that to our ears the difference between the *Ars Antiqua,* the "old art," and the new music of the Vitry era would sound as striking as the difference between Brahms and Stravinsky, for example. (Incidentally, it is entirely possible to enjoy this experience with the aid of an excellent collection of recordings illustrating the history of Western music, under the name of *"Anthologie Sonore."*) Everybody who occupies himself with the history of music will notice that stylistic differences, oftentimes a matter of alarm and heated controversy to the contemporary witnesses, shrink in proportion to the distance in time, so that after only a hundred years or even less we can hardly understand what the shouting was about unless we try consciously to put ourselves into the situation of the contemporary listeners. On the other hand, objectively discernible differences of a technical nature stand out more clearly when the dust has settled.

Throughout the Middle Ages the sacred music of the Gregorian Chant was the center and core of all serious art music. The Chant is, as everybody knows, music of one single melodic line—so to speak, two-dimensional music—in which the tonal substance moves on a surface, as it were, without depth. Polyphony—that is, the simultaneous operation of two or more melodic lines—is a concept entirely peculiar to the mind of Western man. There is some evidence of its having been practiced by some Western European tribes in prehistoric times, but it was introduced into art music only in the tenth century. Yet even this momentous change did not affect the supremacy of the Gregorian Chant. If there were several melodic lines going on at the same time, one of them was always a melody quoted from the Chant, and the other voices were subordinate acolytes. Consequently these additional voices, which originally were thought of as a background adding depth and profile to the sacred melody, would behave in ways similar to those of the Chant.

Without going too far into technical detail, let us focus on just one of the most important characteristics of the Chant. Its oldest melodies are, like the religion itself that it served, of Oriental origin, and later additions were fashioned after those models. What distinguishes these melodies most conspicuously from the indigenous music of the West is the fact that their points of emphasis, or accents, are irregularly distributed over phrases of varying lengths. Thinking of any European folk-tune that may come to our minds, we can easily verify that in such a tune the several sections of the melody, its phrases, are of equal length, which causes the accents to occur at equal intervals, that is, to be spaced regularly, as in marching or dancing tunes. This condition reminds us of versified poetry in which the corresponding lines have the same number of syllables and accents, while the structure of the Chant's melodies is more akin to that of prose, which is well in keeping with the fact that the texts employed in the Chant, mainly taken from the Old Testament, were freely articulated prose.

To give the gist of the processes that make up the history of occidental music: one might say that it has consisted chiefly in a constant interplay of these opposing principles, and that the wealth and variety of musical forms of expression in our civilization are due to ever renewed approaches to the problem of reconciling and integrating these two forces; the square, symmetrical structure of Western, secular music, and the free articulation of the soaring, floating melodic lines emanating from the Eastern sources of the Chant.

The considerable quantity of sacred music that has come down to us through the ages, if compared to that of secular music, seems to suggest that secular music was a rather unimportant factor in mediaeval life. This certainly is not correct, for worldly music was created and used continuously on a large scale. It is true, however, that the composers put

forth their most conscientious efforts in the writing of religious music, and that the most interesting, elaborate, and
forward-looking accomplishments were obtained in that
field.

Polyphonic Procedure

R ETURNING now to the Ars Nova of the fourteenth century,
we may point out as one of its salient characteristics a
certain infiltration of elements from the worldly sector.
What this amounts to can be most easily comprehended if it
is visualized in technical terms. We realize that the average
reader is, for some reason or other, afraid of nothing so
much as of technical terms of music, although he has long
ago become quite used to the elementary shop-language of
sports, medicine, physics, aviation, military science, and
other subject matters dealt with in the daily news. Of course
musical terms are by no means more difficult to understand
than those of other fields, and all of them can be elucidated
in plain language.

When two or more melodies are progressing simultaneously, one of the chief problems is timing their progress
properly, so that they will reach at the same time the points
of coincidence planned by the composer. As long as the task
of polyphonic (that is, "multi-voiced") composition consisted in adding one voice to the given melody of the Gregorian Chant, the timing problem was relatively simple. Two
possibilities were available, in order to assure a well-coordi-
nated progress of the two melodies. Either the added voice
would proceed at the same pace as the given voice—that is,
each tone of the Chant melody would be combined with one
tone of the new voice, so that both would have the same

number of tones—or the duration of the individual tones of the Chant melody would be extended to considerable length and the other, new voice would be made to produce a great number of tones of short duration against each of the long-drawn-out tones of the Chant. Both procedures were actually employed, the second one somewhat later in the evolution of this kind of writing, when the possibilities of the earlier technique ("note against note") became too limited for the expressive desires of the composer.

As soon as two or even three voices were added to the Chant—a temptation to which the composers of the Notre Dame School in Paris yielded in the twelfth and thirteenth centuries—the problems of coordination of those voices grew more complex. Again, the composers resorted at first to organizing the polyphonic fabric so that the added voices would move together in fairly short, easily controllable phrases. The result was the typical style of the Ars Antiqua, which because of its simplicity of texture in its best moments showed majestic grandeur, but at length became somewhat clumsy and monotonous. It is here that the Ars Nova opened up new possibilities in that it gave to the additional voices a higher degree of internal variety in rhythm and of independence from each other in regard to simultaneous motion. The voices now began to use more interesting sequences of tones of different durations, and also they would not any longer stop and go at the same time. One might say that this development marks the beginning of real polyphony as a lively and variegated interplay of voices, each moving according to its own melodic impulse and all of them coordinated by the masterplan of counterpoint.

For this is, by the way, how we can, for practical purposes, distinguish polyphony and counterpoint: Polyphony is any kind of ensemble music making, in which several melodic lines are progressing simultaneously. Counterpoint is the set of principles which regulates the sound combinations arising at any given point on account of the simultaneous progress of those voices. Obviously those principles are not rigidly fixed—they are set up by man in accordance with his aesthetic likes and dislikes, which in turn depend upon the general disposition of his mind. Thus the principles of counterpoint have changed throughout history ever since the beginning of polyphony, so that what was accepted as a satisfactory procedure in the fourteenth century differs in many points from the precepts applied by Palestrina and his kinsmen of style in the sixteenth, just as the counterpoint of Bach is different from the ideas entertained by twentieth-century composers.

If we surmise that the composers of the Ars Nova were tempted to introduce greater liveliness and subtlety of rhythmic subdivision into their sacred works under the influence of the charming noises emanating from the flower gardens of secular music, we are supported in this conjecture by the fact that these composers also turned more frequently to doing some pleasure gardening of their own than had their predecessors of the Ars Antiqua. Both great masters of the Ars Nova, Guillaume Machault in France and Francesco Landini in Italy, and many smaller ones, left an important array of chansons and madrigals—thas is, vocal compositions of a secular nature. Modern scholars were so impressed by this fact that they saw in it the first stirrings of the spirit of the Renaissance in music.

Middle Ages and Renaissance

THE question as to when the mediaeval manners of musical creation came to an end and gave way to the attitudes of the Renaissance is a controversial one. In general history the line of demarkation between the Middle Ages and the

Modern Age is conventionally drawn at 1492, the year in which the last stronghold of the Arabs on the European continent, Granada, was conquered by the Spaniards, and the New World of the Western hemisphere was discovered by Columbus. This is, of course, too mechanical and specific a line of division if one wishes to describe the subtle and gradual changes in the disposition of the mind of occidental man which are manifest enough to prompt us into assuming the existence of two different phases of history.

As far as music history is concerned, the divergence in opinion is so great that the older school of historians, especially the German musicologists of the nineteenth century, are inclined to include even Palestrina among the musical mediaevalists, although he died a hundred years after the discovery of America, while more recent scholars, like the American Gustave Reese, date the end of the Middle Ages in music around 1400. This difference of nearly two hundred years in the evaluation of historical evidence does not suggest that the experts are incompetent, because they do not seem to know what they are talking about, but only underlines the fact that the answer to such questions depends entirely on the criteria applied, and that such criteria change according to the perspective of the observer of history, which perspective in turn is a result of his position in the historical process. The problem deserves our attention because Ockeghem's life unfolded within that contested period of two hundred years, and we should like to know how to place him in relation to the Middle Ages and the Renaissance.

If the older viewpoint is accepted, there is little left in the history of music that could be described as music of the Renaissance. For the new style that emerged soon after Palestrina already shows so many characteristics of the Baroque that it ought to be considered a part of that stylistic area. In fact some scholars, like Cecil Gray, are inclined to think that music somehow has skipped the phase of the Renaissance, that there actually was no such thing as Renaissance music. They base their reasoning on the notion that the spirit of the Renaissance was opposed to the very nature of music. In this opinion music is essentially a romantic art, a manifestation of the obscure, emotional, fantastic side of human nature, and as such not capable of associating itself with the intellectual, rationalistic, and scientific attitudes that are typical of the Renaissance mind. Consequently music, it is said, had moved directly from the mystical world of the Middle Ages to the exuberance of the Baroque, which is seen as a sort of modern version of the Gothic, without having partaken of the tendencies expressed in the Renaissance.

It seems to us that this view perhaps goes too far, partly because such an analysis tends to overlook the strongly intellectual, constructive, mathematical component in mediaeval art, partly because it does not take into account the element of lucid, rational control of the sound material, the nearly superhuman poise and elegance, which distinguishes the style of Palestrina. Obviously there was no need for the Renaissance to invent the power of reason. Scholasticism, the leading philosophy of the Middle Ages, offers ample proof that logical thinking was as well developed then as at any other time. On the other hand, much of the music of the sixteenth century evinces the fact that the composers were far from indifferent to the ideas of their age which were based on a new, scientific and exploratory attitude toward nature. It is not so much a difference in the intellectual equipment that determines a variety of stylistic aspects in art, but rather a difference in expressive intent. The conflict of emotion versus intellect in art is greatly overrated by observers who do not clearly understand the nature and function of technique in music. A composer who wishes to write passionate operatic arias must know as much about counterpoint as his colleague who devotes himself to religious *a cappella* music. Either one will use his technical abilities with different ends in mind and therefore in different ways. But the mere fact that a motet contains some intricate contrapuntal devices, and thus seems to prove its author to be an "intellectualist," may not prevent it from conveying a much higher degree of expressive intensity than many an operatic scene of extremely simple texture and straightforward appeal, conceived by a typical "emotionalist."

What Makes Ancient Music Sound Ancient?

H OWEVER, if a modern listener had the opportunity of hearing an Ockeghem work right after one by Palestrina, he would probably say that in spite of their individual differences both Ockeghem and Palestrina sounded to him alike because both of them had that typical color of sound which seems to distinguish all "old" music and set it apart from the music of the "modern" era so familiar to our ears. What constitutes this peculiar flavor that is common to all music written before 1600, roughly speaking? It is the idiom in which that music is conceived—the selection of sound combinations predominantly employed and the context into which these sounds are placed, just as the selection and context of linguistic sounds create the unmistakable acoustical flavor which sets one language apart from another.

The idiom of mediaeval music is frequently called modal, but this term has been used so loosely that it hardly conveys any definite meaning unless it is explained. Here again we stand in need of a little technical discussion, brief but indispensable for the understanding of the character of ancient music.

Western music is based on a peculiar selection of tones chosen from the continuum of all possible tones that one might hear, for instance, in the wail of a siren. In that selection the tones follow each other, if arranged according to pitch, in groups of two and three tones each, these tones being separated from each other by a relatively large interval, called a whole-tone step. Between these two groups there is inserted a smaller interval, known as a half-tone. Such a small interval also follows the group of three whole-tone steps, which then is again followed by two whole tones, and so forth. This can be easily verified if the reader will look at the white keys of a piano. There he will find two whole-tone steps, from C to D, and from D to E. Then he will observe a half-tone step, from E to F, and three whole steps, from F to G, to A, to B. Another half step leads to C, and the sequence begins over again, as we say, an octave (that is, eight steps) higher. This corresponds to what is nowadays known as the major scale—in this case the C major scale.

If we now visualize the gamut of an octave as the frame of reference for a melodic process, that is an individual sequence of tones, we can set up such gamuts on each tone of the scale which we just have described. (This scale, by the way, in which the tones follow each other in the order discussed, is called a diatonic scale.) We will have an octave reaching from C to the next higher C, one from D to D, another from E to E, and so forth. It is easy to see that all these octaves contain the same tones. However, they are different in regard to the location of the whole-tone and half-tone steps inside of each octave. For example, in the octave which begins on D, the half-tone steps lie between the second and third (E and F) and the sixth and seventh tones (B and C). When we start out from F, we will encounter half-tone steps between the fourth and fifth (B-C) and the seventh and eighth tones (E and F) of our scale. Obviously there are

31

seven different scales—different, that is, in regard to the lo-cation of the intervals between their tones—available within the diatonic gamut which we have set up. Skipping a few semantic subtleties which are important only if we want to go into a detailed study of the subject, we may dispose of this matter by saying that these seven different scales are described in music theory as modes.

In the ancient music four of these were commonly used as frames of reference for melodic processes, that is, melodies would move characteristically within the orbits of those scales, usually beginning and always ending on the funda-mental tones of the scales, stressing certain other tones ac-cording to the conventions attached to each individual mode, and the like. From these four basic modes, which covered the octave segments of the diatonic row beginning on D, E, F, and G, four auxiliary modes were derived which again contained the same tones and were distinguished from the basic ones through differences in the location of the tones which were to receive emphases in the musical process.

The "Modern" Sound

Does "modern" music—that is, the music after 1600—have any kind of organization which may be compared to the system of modes outlined above? It has indeed. This music, which is the music to which we are accustomed to the extent of not even thinking of the possibility of any other organization, uses as frame of reference two scales, known as major and minor. They, of course, are part of the system of seven octaves which we have just studied, and can easily be identified as those beginning on C and A respectively. It then seems that our music is more limited in its possibilities than the old music, for whereas the ancients molded their material in reference to eight different sets of the elements (four basic plus four auxiliary modes), we are using only two such sets (major and minor modes). Is our music then poorer than mediaeval music? It is in some ways, but we have substituted for the lost modes a powerful device which the ancients practically did not use at all.

So far we have, in this little discussion of the musical material and its organization, disregarded the tones which are produced by the black keys of the piano. Everybody knows that they are abundantly used in our music. What is their function? Among other purposes which we do not have to investigate here, these tones serve us mainly to reproduce the conditions of our two modes on various pitch levels. Let us suppose that we should like to establish a major scale on D. We remember that the project means going up in two whole steps, one half step, three whole steps and winding up with another half step. The first whole step leads from D to E. The second whole step offers a problem, for the next tone in our diatonic scale is F, which is only a half step higher than E. We therefore have to proceed to a tone higher than F, but not to G, which is one and a half tones away from E, in other words too high. The tone which we need lies between F and G, a half tone higher than F and a half tone lower than G. It is known as F sharp and represented by the black key between F and G. F sharp being the third tone of our new scale, we have now to continue with a half step. No new tone is necessary, since the G of our original scale is exactly a half step higher than F sharp. Thus we return to the original scale and go on from G in three whole steps. The first two of them are easy: G to A, A to B. The third confronts us with the same problem which we encountered arriving at E. The next tone in the old scale—C—is too low. We have again to move to the black key above C, known as C sharp. From there a half step leads to D, as required by the pattern of the major mode.

This procedure can be repeated by shifting the major mode to any one of the white keys, and each time another group of the black keys will be put into action. Eventually we can use the black keys too as starting points of major scales, and we shall wind up with a set of twelve major scales, each beginning on one of the twelve different tones which we find within the span on an octave: C, C sharp, D, D sharp, and so forth, up to B. The tone on which such a scale is set up is called "key" (not to be confused with the keys of the piano to which we have referred so frequently). The procedure analysed above is known as "transposing" the major scale onto D. The scale which we have obtained is a "transposition" of the major mode to D. If we hear that a piece is written "in F major," it means that its frame of reference is the major mode beginning on F. The key indicates the pitch level of the mode.

In our music we not only put different pieces of music in different keys to set them apart in mood and general color, but, what is even more important, we let the musical process within a composition wander through different keys, which the technician calls "modulation." This procedure was practically unknown to the ancients. They frequently changed the modal reference in the course of a musical process, but always stayed within the same key. To be sure, they were not unfamiliar with the extra tones represented by the black keys of our piano—in fact, all twelve tones of our octave have theoretically been always known and were used in composition as early as in the Ars Nova of the fourteenth century—which, incidentally, is another token of its progressive tendencies—but these writers employed the extra tones for other purposes than modulation in the modern meaning of the term. Consequently, their music constantly runs through the same tonal combinations, even if they vary the modal

34

reference of them. Their modal variations are more subtle
and inconspicuous than the modern procedures of modulation, and this is why ancient music easily sounds a bit monotonous and colorless to the ears of those accustomed to
the drastic shifts and vivid contrasts so characteristic of
more recent music.

If modal orientation as described above is taken as a typical attribute of mediaevalism, it is not illogical to extend
the reign of the Middle Ages in music as far as Palestrina,
for in his music he still acknowledges that pattern of organization of the musical elements. If one attaches more importance to the deviations from mediaeval attitudes in mood
and content as expressed in the technical innovations of the
Ars Nova, he might be inclined to see in these the first and
decisive manifestations of the spirit of the Renaissance. In
this case a figure like Johannes Ockeghem becomes even
more strange and problematical than it is when considered
independently from historical categories.

The Mass and the Cantus Firmus

As compared to the work of the great masters of the sixteenth century, Palestrina and Orlando di Lasso, Ockeghem's output seems to be disappointingly small. While their
masses and motets are counted by the hundreds or even
thousands, we know of only fifteen masses and seven motets
by Ockeghem, apart from a small number of secular compositions. It is reasonable to assume that he has left many
more religious works than these and that most of his manuscripts were destroyed in Rome, when the holy city was
assaulted by the mutinous troops of Emperor Charles V in
1527.

The Catholic mass, as an object of musical composition, had a relatively brief history when Ockeghem occupied himself with it. Until the fourteenth century only the Gregorian settings of the sacred text were used in the ecclesiastical services. The first example of a polyphonic setting of those words—a three-voice composition without reference to Gregorian melodies—is the so-called "Mass of Tournai," written by one or several anonymous authors some time in the early 1300s. The first composition of that kind that achieved great and justified fame is the four-voice mass by Guillaume Machault, completed around 1360. There appeared a few other specimens in the latter part of the century, but only in the fifteenth-century composing was the mass taken up on a grand scale; and soon it became the central preoccupation of religious composers, which is tantamount to saying: of composers.

The formal pattern which was set up for the composition of the mass has remained valid to this day, regardless of modifications of style, medium, emphasis, etc. The subject matter of those compositions is the "Ordinarium missae," consisting of Kyrie, Gloria, Credo, Sanctus, Benedictus, and Agnus Dei. The first and the last sections are easily divided into three parts, according to the well-known organization of the text. Sanctus and Benedictus are occasionally conceived of as a unit. Gloria, and especially Credo, which offers considerable structural problems because of the extraordinary number of words furnished by the liturgical text, are subdivided according to varying principles. In these sections the intonation is reserved for the priest at the altar, so that the composition starts on the words "Et in terra pax" in the Gloria and "Patrem omnipotentem" in the Credo, respectively.

We have already said that mediaeval composition always revolved around a melody quoted from the Gregorian Chant. The most important type of this kind of musical work was called the *motet,* and the Gregorian melody which was the backbone of those polyphonic settings was known as the *cantus firmus,* "fixed chant." At times this term was supposed to refer to the fact that the book in which the Gregorian melodies were written up was firmly attached with a chain to the lectern in the church in order to protect it from being stolen. A less materialistic meaning seems to be suggested by another term that was used to indicate the role of that melody in the polyphonic fabric: *cantus prius factus,* that is, "chant made beforehand"; in other words, the given melody in relation to which the new, additional voices were constructed.

It is interesting to notice that the early polyphonic compositions of the mass were only partly, or not at all, built around a cantus firmus taken from the chant. We shall not try to answer the obvious question whether this may have been another token of the emancipatory tendencies which characterized various aspects of the Ars Nova. The composers of the fifteenth century, beginning with Guillaume Dufay, almost always employed cantus firmi in their settings of the mass, but only rarely were these selected from the melodic treasures of the Gregorian Chant. More frequently the "given melodies" are secular songs, either folk-tunes of more or less anonymous origin, or art songs written by contemporary secular composers or those of a slightly earlier generation—once in a while even by the religious composers themselves.

A Disconcerting Practice

THIS practice certainly appears to us strange, and even disconcerting. The songs which were used were of a pronouncedly secular character, especially in regard to the texts, and they were well-known popular songs, undoubtedly serving purposes very similar to those of the entertainment music of our time. We would surely find it shocking if nowadays a composer should write a mass over the cantus firmus "Begin the Beguine" or "The Blue Danube Waltz." Not only the church authorities, but everybody else would throw up their hands in horror. However, that was exactly the case when fifteenth-century composers wrote masses around such tunes as "Se la face ay pale" or "Malheur me bat," sentimental, passionate, or whimsical love songs.

Naturally this practice has provoked a great deal of comment. One attempt at explaining it was the conjecture that those composers wanted to make their works more palatable to the listeners by weaving some well-known melodies into the complicated polyphonic fabric of their masses. It was assumed that the average listener was unable to derive much satisfaction from the intricate texture of the multi-voiced ensemble, that he was in no position to appreciate the learned contrapuntal procedures and intellectual "artifices" of the style, and that he would feel somehow comforted if he could identify a familiar tune in the bewildering interplay of the voices.

This explanation does not seem quite plausible for various reasons. In the first place the cantus firmi in those masses are treated in such ways that it appears very unlikely that they could be perceived and followed easily by the audience. They are never carried by the top voice, the soprano, which naturally attracts the immediate attention of the listener. In most cases they are located in the third voice (from top) of the usual four-part setting, which is the tenor. Nowadays we associate the term "tenor" with the high male voice, as distinguished from the intermediate quality of the baritone and the low one of the bass. Originally, however, "tenor," derived from the Latin verb *tenere* ("to hold"), is by definition the voice which "holds" the cantus firmus, and thus the whole musical edifice. Occasionally, but rarely, the cantus firmus will appear in the bass, as in Ockeghem's *Missa Caput*. In any case, this location makes the cantus firmus rather imperceptible for the average listener.

Furthermore, the cantus firmus always proceeds in long, sometimes extremely long, notes, while the other voices are occupied with frequently very lively motion in much shorter notes, another circumstance that stands in the way of easy perception of the cantus firmus. If under such conditions the composer had wanted the cantus firmus to be heard, he would have had to have it supported by some heavy instrumental combination, such as strong organ registers and brass instruments. It stands to reason that the cantus firmus was brought out with some instrumental support, or perhaps even on instruments alone, since it would have been nearly impossible for singers to hold its very long tones. However, it is unlikely that the composer would have favored an arrangement by which the cantus would drown out the contrapuntal activity of the other voices in which the entire interest of the composition was concentrated, and which was the artistic excuse for the whole undertaking.

Furthermore, the conjecture that secular cantus firmi were chosen in order to please the listeners is hardly acceptable, because it is based on applying modern views of audience psychology to the totally different mediaeval situation. There are many reasons for assuming that not only was the mediaeval composer of religious music not concerned with

39

the people who heard his music during the ecclesiastical services, but that nobody conceived of these people as what we today call an "audience." We remember that on a trip through Spain our attention was drawn, in one of the magnificent Gothic cathedrals of the fifteenth century, to a particularly interesting work of sculpture tucked away high up under the vault of the nave. It was brought out by a special searchlight and had to be inspected with the aid of binoculars. When we asked the priest who acted as a guide why so important an object was placed so that it hardly could be seen by the worshippers, he answered with great simplicity and dignity: "It was not put there to be beheld by man, but as an offering to God, who can see it wherever it might be."

Anyone who makes a penetrating study of mediaeval polyphony must come to the conclusion that these composers were activated by a similar conception of the function of their art in the universe. They certainly did not intend to entertain the congregation with pleasant sound combinations, and no one expected them to do so. They tried to muster the resources of their art in order to achieve the highest degree of perfection that was at their disposal, and thus to please God, for whom nothing less than the most elaborate and demanding artistic creation would do.

A positive answer to the question why, under these circumstances, the composers felt like using such frivolous tunes as points of departure for their lofty constructions can not be given with a satisfactory degree of assurance. Since the contrapuntal voices which were added to the cantus firmus, and constituted the real artistic achievement involved in those compositional projects, followed the free, floating articulation characteristic of the ever changing accent pattern of the Gregorian Chant, it would have seemed more than logical to choose as cantus firmi, melodies of the same character that apparently was desirable in the invention of the new, additional voices—that is, melodies from the Chant. However, that was done only rarely, as mentioned before. One might say that these composers perhaps unconsciously obeyed the historical law according to which occidental music was ordained to develop, namely by intertwining those opposite components, the oriental one, of free articulation, and the occidental one, of symmetrical scanning, which we have discussed earlier. From a purely technical point of view of composition the decision to use those secular tunes appears to be sound enough. The worldly cantus firmi with their well-defined, clear-cut phrases provided an excellent frame of reference for the articulation of larger musical forms which were demanded by the considerable extension of the sacred texts of the mass. And such clear articulation was obviously a problem of paramount importance, since the artistic will was directed toward a boundlessly floating and streaming interplay of independent voices.

Even if these premises are acknowledged, there remains the question why the composers did not make up some suitable cantus firmi without secular connotation, instead of introducing tunes which on account of the lyrics that were originally attached to them might have offended the religious feelings of anybody who became aware of their background. Here again a definite explanation is hardly possible. It could be said that the mediaeval tradition of erecting a musical edifice upon the cornerstone of a "cantus prius factus" was so strong that the composers would rather employ a cantus in spite of its objectionable textual connotation than get along without such a "given melody." We have to admit that, after everything is said and done, there remains an irrational element in this practice which must be left unresolved.

The Cantus Firmus Technique

How does the cantus firmus technique operate practically? The answer is very simple: the tune chosen as a cantus firmus is repeated throughout the whole composition as many times as the length of the work requires it. Since, as was pointed out before, the cantus moves along in very long notes, not too many repetitions are necessary. In the shorter sections of the mass, like the Kyrie, Sanctus, and Benedictus, often not the entire cantus is employed, but perhaps only its opening two or three phrases. After each phrase of the cantus, the tenor voice which carries it has an unspecified number of rests, during which the other voices continue their independent contrapuntal work. The cantus does not always appear in the same rhythmic shape. At times its pace is faster, then again slower. If the time value of its notes is reduced to shorter ones, we speak of "diminution." The opposite process is known as "augmentation."

There are other, more subtle modifications of the cantus, which already belong to the province of the much vaunted "artifices." It may be that only certain tones of the cantus—according to some premeditated pattern that affects perhaps every other, or every third tone, or such—are changed in regard to their duration. Once in a while it may also happen that the cantus appears in "inversion," that is, the direction of its melodic progressions is inverted. Where the original melody moves upward, the inversion will move downward, while the length of the respective intervals remains the same, and vice versa. In some rare cases the retrograde form of the cantus, or of some of its phrases, is utilized, which means that the last tone of the original phrase becomes the first, so that the whole phrase is read backwards. These variants are, of course, much too subtle to be perceived by the listener. They only serve the composer in deriving new ideas of design from the new aspects of his basic material, which are furnished by those modifications.

One may ask the question, What practical purpose is accomplished by clinging to such a cantus firmus throughout the whole length of an extended composition, if the listener is admittedly unable to follow by ear the involved operations of that technique? The answer is that the cantus firmus lends structural unity to the work, since its repeated occurrence will more or less automatically lead to the recurrence of similar situations and thus vouchsafe consistency of the compositional context. Of course it can be asserted that the composers could have achieved this aim, if they wanted to, without using a somewhat mechanical-looking device. In fact, they did so from time to time when they wrote a mass which traditionally carried the subtitle *sine nomine* ("without name"), in which no cantus firmus was employed. However, in the majority of cases they preferred to accomplish their intentions by entrusting the unity of the work to the powers of a cantus prius factus, and this we have to accept as a fact.

The usual number of voices in Ockeghem's masses is four, although there are a few with only three voices. Writing for five voices became customary in the latter part of the fifteenth century. The Kyrie always begins with the full number of voices. Its middle section, "Christe eleison," then has frequently only three voices, leaving out the cantus firmus, which returns in the final "Kyrie eleison." The Gloria and Credo nearly always begin with two voices, and the two opening sections of these movements are closely related to each other through the use of similar motivic material. These motives are oftentimes clearly derived from characteristic features of the cantus firmus. In those long movements of the mass we find again an alternation of sections that employ the total number of voices with sections of a thinner texture. In the remaining parts of the mass—Sanctus, Benedictus, and Agnus Dei—the two-voice opening is again the rule, but occasionally the arrangements are different.

Melody and Rhythm

T HE melodic motion of the added voices is relatively simple. They progress mainly in stepwise motion, that is, from one tone of the scale to the next. Skips are used sparingly, so that their expressive effect is rather telling. The "extra tones" discussed earlier—those represented by the black keys of the piano—are very rare. As a rule they appear only as modifications of the "natural" tones in the approach to phrase endings: when, for instance, a phrase ends on G and this tone is approached from the F below it, this F is raised to F sharp. There are a few other situations in which such "extra" tones may appear, but we do not have to concern ourselves here with such details.

If the melodic motion of the voices, that is their moving from pitch to pitch, does not seem to reveal any startling characteristics, their progress in time is the more interesting. It is in fact in this field that the amazing and unique properties of Ockeghem's music became manifest. As we have mentioned earlier, the contrapuntal voices which made up the polyphonic fabric woven around the cantus firmus were conceived in the spirit of the melodic conception of the Gregorian Chant, which throughout the Middle Ages remained the ideal for which melodic invention in art music was forever striving. Those melodies were different from those of the Chant in that they contained a great variety of time values, that is, notes of different duration. While the

Chant knew basically only of two categories of notes, short and long—the long note usually doubling the duration of the short one—the melodies of the polyphonic composers employed notes of which the longest could easily be sixteen times as long as the shortest, with all intermediate values available at any time.

The polyphonic melodies were similar to those of the Chant in that they too had the same floating, unearthly quality, freely suspended, as it were, in the musical space without the audible support of a preconceived regular accent pattern. For us who have been steeped in the tradition of regularly scanning, symmetrical music it is very difficult to conceive this condition clearly, and this difficulty, by the way, is a serious obstacle when attempts are made at a correct rendition of mediaeval music in our day. One of the chief problems of composition in the Middle Ages was to reconcile the evasive quality of the melodies with the requirement of precise timing, indispensable in polyphonic music, and the methods by which this problem was solved are responsible for the unique make-up of mediaeval music, for its astounding complexity, and its peculiar difficulty.

In order to get a clear picture of the situation, we have to analyse the significance of the fact that this music was written without barlines. At first glance this may seem to be a trifle, a graphical detail of subordinate, purely technical importance. We are so used to the barlines in our modern music that we are apt to forget what they really mean. Of course they are signposts by which the musicians can tell where they are. The conductor is supposed to give a downbeat after every barline, and from that the various executants of an ensemble piece can tell when they have to come in. If in a rehearsal of chamber music something goes wrong, the first violinist, or the pianist, will cry "Let's start two bars after 50," and everybody knows where that is. However, the barlines also demonstrate the placement of the recurrent, regular accent, for every tone that stands immediately after a barline receives a dynamic stress, or rather is expected to receive such a stress. In more elaborate pieces of music, which are not simple marching tunes or waltzes or the like, the dynamic stresses are frequently transferred to different parts of the measure, and much of the interest that such music may arouse stems from the fact that the dynamic stresses, or accents, do not occur where they are expected to stand. But the premise of such an experience is the tacit assumption that there is a regular meter in which the accents are distributed at recurring time intervals, like *one*-two, *one*-two-three, *one*-two-three-four, and so forth.

No such thing exists in mediaeval music. Every melodic phrase unfolds according to its own law, without any tone being automatically thrown into relief on account of a pre-existing accent pattern. Essentially all tones of the phrase are dynamically alike, but the long and high tones stand out by virtue of their being long and high, and thus gain weight, so that the articulation of the phrase is a result of the grouping of its tones around such points of emphasis.

The Intricacies of the Mensural System

IN ORDER to keep these freely floating voices together, the mediaeval mind contrived a system of measurement which is as ingenious as it seems involved to us. It can be best explained by suggesting that those musicians thought of music as moving in three layers, each of which was characterized by a certain typical average speed of motion, like three platforms revolving around the same axis at different speeds. The slowest of these was called *modus*, the medium one *tempus*, and the fastest *prolatio*. Theoretically these three terms specified the relations between various note values. Depending on what modus was indicated by certain symbols corresponding to what is now known as time signature, the musician would know into how many notes of a smaller time value each note of the longest type was to be subdivided. Similarly, tempus would express those relations on the next level of the hierarchy, showing the subdivision of the smaller values, and prolatio would do the same in regard to the shortest notes of the system. In practical composition it turned out that the cantus firmus would nearly always stay in the inert region of modus, while the other voices moved on the faster speed levels of tempus and prolatio, often simultaneously partaking of either, or alternating between them, or mixing them in various combinations. This intricate set-up was called the "mensural system," or "mensuration."

As seen from a distance of a few hundred years, the Gothic mind seems to have derived a keen delight from various forms of simultaneity. This is more easily felt when one occupies oneself with the manifestations of that mind than it is described in words. We came closest to experiencing this feeling in a tangible sense when we slowly walked through the apses of some of the elaborate French cathedrals. The more complicated specimens of those vaulted hallways that run around the back of the main altar in a semicircle exhibit three rows of pillars, arranged in concentric circles. Of course the center row of the three has more pillars than the inner one, and the outermost row has more than both of the other rows. All of these pillars are connected by arches, the sinews of which are visible on the ceiling. Naturally the discrepancies in the relative positions of the pillars require a most complex design of arches. Moving slowly through such a hallway, the observer gains with every step a completely new vista, revealing ever changing combinations of lines which result from the varying relationships of radii

47

and peripheries of the three concentric circles. The whole edifice seems to move around him in a mysterious, somewhat astronomic rhythm, with always new and different points emerging as centers of the motion and vanishing again. This visual image may perhaps serve to illustrate the rhythmical conditions of mediaeval music, which we have tried to describe above in technical terms.

This music was called *cantus mensurabilis*, "measured chant," as distinguished from *cantus planus*, "plain chant," by which was, of course, understood the Gregorian Chant. The distinction was based upon the fact that in the polyphonic music, time values were strictly measured, while in the plain chant they were somewhat indefinite and flexible. But as if the procedures of mensuration were not complicated enough, the rhythmic appearance of mediaeval music was further bedeviled by the so-called "proportional system," which ought to be discussed briefly, since Ockeghem made some use of it. At any rate, it belonged to the regular equipment of the composers of that age.

More Complicated: the Proportional System

THE idea behind this tricky device can be best understood when we realize that music in the Middle Ages was thought of as having one single and rather immutable standard speed. The manifold variations of basic tempo which we nowadays are used to expressing in innumerable shadings through a series of Italian adjectives reaching from *Prestissimo* to *Largo* did not then exist. Tempo indications are entirely missing from the manuscripts. Since mediaeval music did not provide for dramatic and drastic contrasts so characteristic of modern music, there was no need for

48

sharply articulated differences in tempo either. But composers developed a desire for subtle variations of the basic speed within the context of a work. According to their manners of thinking, such modifications could be expressed only in relation to the standard speed. The proportional system served the purpose.

If a section of a composition was supposed to move faster, one had to indicate how many notes of a certain type in the faster section would fill the time span taken up by a smaller number of notes of the same type in the preceding portion.

This was done by means of fractions: $\frac{4}{3}$, for instance, would mean that, in the passage following the fraction, four notes would have to be run off in as much time as three notes of the same category absorbed in the passage before the fraction; that is to say, they would be played, or sung, a little faster; to be exact: in the proportion of three to four. With a little mental effort we are able to conceive such a shift in tempo. The situation becomes somewhat more delicate when only one or two voices out of four will partake of the speedup, as frequently happened in mediaeval music when such proportions were applied.

At any rate, three to four is a relatively simple proportion, and it is a certain relief to know that in actual music proportions of this kind were nearly always utilized. However, the fearlessness, one might say recklessness, of the Gothic mind in matters intellectual induced the theorists to work out a most logical and frightfully intricate system of proportions, so that they would not hesitate to discuss in their treatises such hair-raising ratios as thirteen to seven, which would cause nightmares to anybody who would try to carry them out.

It ought to be noticed in passing, that we are using in our time a device which follows the same principle as the proportional system, when we employ metronome markings to indicate the speed of a piece of music. When we write: "quarter notes equal 72," for instance, we mean that in that particular section of the work seventy-two quarter notes should take up sixty seconds. In terms of the proportional system this would be expressed by the ratio of six to five, assuming that sixty beats to a minute were considered the "normal" speed of music. Seen in this light, the idea of the proportional system loses much of its horrifying character.

Ockeghem made very sparing use of this device, and it is due only to his occasional pleasure in contrapuntal intricacies that he has been throughout history accused of having persistently indulged in the more esoteric vices of the proportional system. He was, however, not averse to occasional and frequently startling changes of tempo which he carried out by simply using smaller subdivisions of the standard notes, without resorting to the proportions. In fact, these changes of tempo are so typical of his style that one might call them a trademark of his. The stately, majestic flow of the music is repeatedly disturbed by sudden eddies, real whirlpools of motion, which seemingly come from nowhere, pushed to the surface, as it were, by some hidden groundswell. They disappear as quickly and mysteriously as they have erupted, and at times they are followed by a particularly static, restful passage. This seems to reveal a type of nervous, sensitive imagination not frequently encountered in the music of the period.

The temporary speeding up of the musical process naturally causes accented tones to be crowded together into narrow areas, which creates the precipitous character of those passages. That this effect can be achieved without altering the mensuration scheme of the whole composition should prove the point which we have tried to bring out as one of the most important ones in this discussion: the mensuration—that is, the codification of the relationships between tones of different durations—was meant to be a mechanism for keeping time, and nothing else. It did not involve any metric considerations, that is, it did not regulate the placement of dynamic stresses, or accents. These were entirely a result of the musical process itself which created its accent pattern as it went along, without any premeditated regularity. Consequently the true nature of this music comes to light only when it is transcribed in modern notation without barlines.

Problems of Notation

THIS brief sentence seems to raise a number of questions. Why has this music to be "transcribed" at all? Was it originally written in a notation different from ours? Has it been transcribed with barlines, and if so, why? We shall endeavor to answer these questions one by one.

The graphic symbols in which this music was laid down are indeed different from those which we are using today. They are known as "mensural notation." The notes are similar to our modern notes, which were gradually developed from the symbols of mensural notation, except that the mensural system uses rectangular, square, and diamond-shaped notes to indicate various time values. The main difference between the old system and the new is that in the old one a note which may be subdivided into two smaller ones looks exactly the same as a note that may be divided into three smaller values. One can tell the difference only by referring to the code which is put in front of the staff. In the modern system every note is normally divisible into two notes of the next smaller order. A whole note has two half notes, a half note has two quarter notes, and so forth. If a longer note should be divided into three, we add a dot to it, to indicate that it is lengthened by 50% of its original duration. A dotted half note has three quarter notes, and so on.

It is interesting to notice that in the ancient system the subdivision into three was considered the norm. It was called "perfect." A subdivision into two was conceived of as a result of cutting off something from the perfect condition, and therefore was called "imperfect." Again we see that the "threeness" was felt to be the norm of perfection. Some historians suggest that this was a reflection of the perfection of God, as evidenced in the mystery of the Holy Trinity.

Anyone who has an inkling of the methods of musical notation might remark here that it would not matter too much whether a note which included three smaller notes looked like one which included only two, for in a score one can tell immediately which is which by looking at the next staff. What is a score? A score is a document in which every sound that occurs in a piece of music is recorded in such a way that the reader can tell immediately not only what voice or instrument should produce the sound, but also what sounds should be produced at the same time. Each voice is written on a separate line, and the sounds that should come out simultaneously are written underneath each other. This makes the survey of the most complex musical processes rather easy.

No Scores—No Barlines

HOWEVER, mediaeval music was not written in scores, but
but only in parts. The manuscripts that have come
down to us show what every voice had to sing on separate
sheets, or in different places on the same sheet, but they do
not contain any record of the whole in the form of a score.
Apparently this music was not performed under the direction of a conductor in the modern sense of the term, and
therefore a score was not needed for purposes of performance. Since it is practically inconceivable that a composer
could have contrived a formidable contrapuntal network of
four voices by writing them out on four different sheets,
without ever seeing in one place how these voices fitted together, it has recently been suggested by scholars that the
composer actually did write a score, but probably only as a
sketch. In those days writing material was scarce and pre-
cious, and so it seems that these scores were written on some
kind of tablets which could be wiped clean, after the individual parts were extracted, and used again for another
work. These conditions changed at the end of the fifteenth
century, and in the sixteenth century we already find scores
of the type which has ever since remained customary.

The difficulties encountered in performing this music
must have been staggering. Every interpreter of modern
chamber music knows how many "accidents" occur during
the first readings of such scores, how many cues are missed,
and how often the musicians have to stop because somebody
"got lost." And yet, orientation in such works is relatively
easy because the players can always refer to the barlines and
take up their study at any point of the work they desire. A
singer of mediaeval polyphonic music had nothing to rely

upon except his ability to keep time accurately. Once he started singing he could only follow his own part, hold every note and every rest faithfully, and use utmost concentration on his work in order to remain undisturbed by the rhythmic vagaries of the other voices, hoping that everybody else would do the same, so that the delicate and fanciful lacework of the polyphonic fabric would stay together. It is true that many other problems with which the modern performer has to cope did not exist for the mediaeval singers, and the music with which they were confronted was all of the same character and offered consistently the same tasks. Nonetheless a formidable training must have been necessary to prepare the performers for their assignments.

In our brief account of Ockeghem's life we could see that he began his musical career as a singer. In those days the field of music was not yet divided into so many special sectors as it is today, and a man who wanted to be a musician received an all-round musical education that covered theory as well as performance. If it was a matter of routine that a composer was able to sing or play various instruments, it was equally true that a performer was well acquainted with the current procedures of musical composition. The singers undoubtedly knew as much about counterpoint as the composers. Otherwise they would not have been able to indulge in a practice known as *supra librum cantare*, "to sing over the book." In this exercise the singers looked together at a cantus firmus in the "book" (probably the collection of Gregorian melodies), and each improvised a counterpoint to the cantus according to the rules he knew. It is hard to believe that the results were particularly satisfactory aesthetically, but that was probably not the purpose of this pastime. It certainly trained the singers in absorbing through personal active experience the peculiarities of the polyphonic style which they were to execute in their professional capacity.

Problems of Performance; Text; Modern Transcription

SPEAKING of the performance practice of the period, we may touch upon the question of instrumental participation. Until the later nineteenth century the only "old" music fairly well known was music of the sixteenth century, especially the works of Palestrina. It was an established fact that this music was performed "a cappella," that is by voices without the cooperation or accompaniment of instruments. This led to the assumption that all ancient music was conceived in this manner. Recent studies have cast considerable doubt on this conjecture. Mediaeval paintings whose subject matter is scenes in which music-making is going on give us some hints as to the participation of instruments in such ensembles. But the products of a painter's fancy can not of course be taken as documentary evidence. From the musical records alone we can not tell whether any instruments were used, nor if so, which ones, and when and what they played. In the reconstructions of mediaeval music which were made under the supervision of Curt Sachs for the aforementioned collection of discs, *"Anthologie Sonore,"* conspicuous use is made of instruments, particularly of brass in Machault's Mass. The effect of those rough and harsh-sounding instruments is fairly startling. Whether this or any other "reconstruction" of surmised original arrangements is correct is anybody's guess. Probably it will never be possible to establish certainty in this matter.

We are not much better informed on the treatment of the texts in those masses. The manuscripts usually show only the first few words of a section of text at the beginning of the corresponding musical passage, without coordinating syllables and notes in the usual manner. When the Gloria begins, the manuscript shows the words "Et in terra," and after a considerable number of musical phrases we find the entry "Laudamus," and so forth. Whether it was left to the discretion of the singers how they would distribute the well-known words among the notes, or whether certain conventions in regard to this procedure were taken for granted, we do not know. It seems, at any rate, that a rather cavalier treatment of the text became customary, for it was one of the many points of criticism raised at the Council of Trent, in the middle of the sixteenth century, against the prevailing practices of ecclesiastical music, that the sacred texts were badly mauled by the singers and that the congregation could not understand the words.

When in the nineteenth century historians began to explore the vast hidden treasures of ancient music, they were faced with the problem of transcribing it into modern notation, for reading the mensural notation requires protracted studies which only trained musicological experts can be expected to carry out. Furthermore, the mensural notation does not lend itself readily to the modern type of score, which had to be used in order to make the music intelligible to present-day musicians. Unfortunately the scholars who prepared the modern editions of that music went one step further than necessary in their attempts toward making the music intelligible. They not only transcribed the mensural notes in modern shape, which did not affect the time values of the original notes, they also supplied barlines at regular intervals, which seriously distorted the character of the music in that it suggests to the reader who is accustomed to the modern function of barlines a metric organization completely foreign to mediaeval music.

Obviously these editors confused the codes of the mensural system with modern time signatures, taking it somehow for granted that the indications of measurement which appear at the beginnings of any piece of music meant the same in ancient music as in modern. The various symbols which were used in the Middle Ages express only relationships of time values. They indicate into how many smaller values any longer note should be subdivided on the various levels of mensuration in a particular musical area. This was necessary since, as we have explained earlier, the notes looked alike, regardless of the principle of subdivision applied in each case. The symbols, however, do not indicate implicitly how many notes of any category ought to be perceived as a metric unit.

The modern time signature functions only in this latter sense. It does not have to say anything about subdivision of time values, for our concept of time relationship is so rationalized that any quarter note anywhere has two eighth notes, any eighth note two sixteenths, and so forth. If we write $\frac{4}{4}$ at the beginning of a piece of music, we do not mean to point out especially that in that piece a whole note would carry four quarter notes, since this is self-evident. What we do mean is that any group of four quarter notes should be considered a metric unit, with a dynamic stress falling systematically on every first note of such a unit. Undoubtedly the use of barlines in the modern editions of ancient music has obstructed a clear understanding of its true character. If one omits the barlines—as we have done in some of our own transcriptions for study purposes—an entirely different and rather surprising picture of that music emerges.

Ockeghem and Dissonance

T HE third important aspect of Ockeghem's music—after the melodic and rhythmic conditions have been discussed —is the harmonic one. The term "harmonic" is used here only as an abbreviation for "the aspect of the sounds produced at any given moment by the simultaneously progressing voices." The modern term "harmony" does not really apply to those sounds, for those sounds were not experienced in the Middle Ages as chords, but as combinations of intervals. (The ancient theorists frequently used the term "harmonia," but by that they understood all sorts of things— even melody!—except what we understand by harmony.) The difference is this: when we hear three tones at once, for instance, C-E-G, we experience that sound as a unit, of a psychological quality distinguished from that of any of its component parts. This new quality is described by the modern term "chord." For the mediaeval musician (and listener) those three tones merely represented a combination of intervals: two thirds (C-E and E-G) and a fifth (C-G).

Everybody knows, and it has been known at all times, that the sounds of simultaneously produced tones—we call them briefly "intervals" and distinguish them by the distance in pitch between the two tones—have different qualities. Some of them sound smooth and even, others harsh and tense. As the science of acoustics teaches us, these differences are due to the fact that the sound waves produced by each tone collide while progressing through the air, which vibrates faster under the impact of the higher of the two tones than under that of the lower one. If the collisions occur at regular distances, as for example in the interval of the octave, in which the number of vibrations of the higher tone is exactly double that of the lower tone, the sound appears to be smooth and reposeful. When the vibration ratio is more complicated, the collisions of the two sound waves are irregularly spaced, which makes the sound comparatively harsh and tense. A gradual increase of harshness and tension may be observed when we proceed from the perfectly smooth interval of the octave through those of the fifth, the fourth, the sixth, and so on, to the so-called minor second (B-C, for instance), which shows the highest measurable amount of tension.

The ancient Greeks with their keen sense for rational order drew an arbitrary line and classified the relatively smooth intervals on one side as consonances, while the intervals on the other side of the line were known as dissonances. Mediaeval theorists who held Greek philosophy in high respect retained this static view. Living music, however, has not always conformed to the precepts of theory, which were frequently based upon postulates of logical reasoning rather than on sensitive observation of the flexible demands of musical expression. In early polyphonic music all kinds of intervals, sharp and mild, tense and relaxed, were used promiscuously. It was the theorists who insisted on discrimination and order, promoting a musical practice in which the consonant intervals would prevail as the norm, while dissonances would be limited to conditional appearances in well-defined places in the musical process.

In this field the history of mediaeval music is characterized by progressive domestication of dissonance. Complete victory was achieved in the thoroughly controlled, rational style of Palestrina in the sixteenth century. After that, dissonance began to counterattack, and the history of modern music is identical with the emancipation of dissonance. At present we have reached the point where the static discrimination between consonance and dissonance has given way to a flexible, relativistic recognition of varying tensions of intervals, which is well in keeping with the new thought patterns in the physical sciences.

In the latter part of the fifteenth century theorists were already far advanced toward doctrines advocating strict and careful control of the use of dissonances. Among other treatises on the subject the *Liber de arte contrapuncti* ("Book on the Art of Counterpoint") by Johannes Tinctoris is a most important piece of evidence. Tinctoris was a compatriot of Ockeghem's, born in Belgium in 1446. He spent most of his later life in the service of the popes in Italy, where he died in 1511. His manual on counterpoint was written in 1477. Tinctoris has very definite ideas on the use of dissonances, which may be somewhat facetiously summed up by saying that he was mainly "against it." He is quite outspoken in his criticism of "ancient" music, because in his opinion early composers were too careless in throwing around their dissonances. He goes as far as to say that decent music worthy of being heard by civilized people had been composed only during the forty years preceding his writing.

It is rather astounding to hear from a scholar and critic so sweeping an indorsement of modern music. Obviously he felt that the composers who had emerged in those forty years shared and practiced in their works his own views on how to put dissonance on a leash. Since he professes to be a close personal friend, keen student and admirer of Ockeghem—with the exception of one or two mild reprimands directed at the composer for having trespassed against some of Tinctoris' precepts—we should have reason to suppose that Ockeghem's music is a prize example of that "decent" modern style which Tinctoris recommends so warmly. It is most surprising, therefore, to discover that actually Ockeghem did not at all live up to the theoretical demands of his friend. In the *Hamline Studies of Musicology*[1] we have devoted an extensive study to the subject and found no expla-

[1] Vol. II, St. Paul, Minn., 1947.

nation for the strange discrepancy. In fact, Ockeghem's music is so permeated by a highly unorthodox treatment of dissonances that this may well be called one of the outstanding features of his style. It endows his music with a unique flavor of rugged melancholy and brings about situations of strength and intensity of feeling not easily found elsewhere.

To our ears this independence in handling dissonances makes Ockeghem's music sound bold and progressive, and in a deeper sense it undoubtedly has a forward-looking perspective, as he exploits the tensions of dissonant combinations in an unconventional way. Nonetheless it is likely that many of his contemporaries found his style archaic, perhaps even obsolete. The fantastic design of his far-flung melodic lines, the abrupt juxtapositions of fast and slow passages, the roughness of his dissonances—all of which, if it occurred in a work of our own time, would earn it the epithet "expressionistic"—was reminiscent of an earlier status of Gothicism in music, which the "modernists" of the period hopefully claimed to have overcome. They already sensed the dawn of the musical ideals of the Renaissance: complete rational control of all musical resources, equilibrium, poise, elegance, polished perfection. The procedures which Tinctoris recommends essentially anticipate the principles according to which, some sixty years later, Palestrina and other great masters worked. In Tinctoris' book the simple and lucid rules of sixteenth-century counterpoint sound involved and a little obscure because he had to explain them in terms of the still prevailing rhythmic complexity and metric boundlessness of polyphonic music. When these conditions were simplified in later practice, everything became clear and uncomplicated.

The strange position of Ockeghem reveals the dialectics of history. Progress in his day meant moving toward higher regularity, greater simplicity of diction and stronger discipline in the use of the more aggressive, fantastic elements of music. Ideals of a classical type—as opposed to those commonly known as romantic—were in the making. Since we are more familiar with a phase of history in which music was moving mainly in the other direction, and composers' efforts were bent on conquering greater freedom in expressive intensity and a more liberal interpretation of traditional principles, we instinctively sense progressive boldness in a composer who uses extreme resources in a manner that seems to indicate his reaching out for unknown quantities.

A similar case in modern times may illustrate the situation, as it is relatively well known: Johann Sebastian Bach, in whom we certainly recognize that genuine boldness of genius which keeps his music alive through the ages, was at the end of his life considered a venerable relic of bygone times, a great master of a hopelessly obsolete style, because music at that time was moving toward the new simplicity of the *gallant style.* The early works of that style appear to us today as childish prattle if we compare them with the awe-inspiring masterworks of the lonely giant of Leipzig. However, we should not blame his contemporaries too severely because it looked different to them.

Relentless Continuity

THE last aspect of Ockeghem's style of composition to be considered is the structural. How did he go about constructing the large musical forms demanded by the extension in time of the texts of the mass? Here again we recognize the dialectical position of this composer. The general taste of the period developed toward musical structures of clearly articulated sections, consisting of well-defined phrase units. The concept of musical form moved away from the perpetuous quality of the Gregorian melody and approached features more typical of secular music. Again Ockeghem seems to cling to the ideals of the past rather than embrace the new. In fact he adheres to the mediaeval concepts more faithfully and with more uncompromising consequence than his predecessors. His musical diction is distinguished by an unusual and at times bewildering continuity.

Just as his melodic phrases seem to be suspended in mid-air because of the indefinite, ever shifting, and unpredictable location of their points of emphasis, so his music rolls on for long stretches without clearly discernible stopping points. Whenever some of the wide-arched melodic strands seem to have run out of their unbelievable energy, and to be approaching a resting point, new ones, generated imperceptibly just before that point is reached, manifest themselves, and the musical process is tirelessly carried forth over another extended area. It is as if a very long bridge were to be built without pillars; each time a span was completed, at the point where a supporting pillar would normally be required, some miraculous engineering device would cause another span to issue from it, and thus the process would continue until the opposite shore was reached.

A particularly striking example of this unique procedure is a long two-voice passage in the *Missa De plus en plus*. It covers what in modern terms would correspond to sixteen measures of six beats each. In it the two melodies, each having about 120 notes, are bouncing and vibrating along like two steel cables stretched out over an abyss, without coming to repose before the final point is reached. The passage, which looks deceptively simple on paper, is so peppered with rhythmic and metric intricacies that even a reader well acquainted with the complications of modern music will get out of breath and fall off the tight-rope several times when he tries to read through it fluently.

Undoubtedly Ockeghem's vision of the large musical form

as an endlessly floating continuum is one of the main causes of the difficulties which beset performance as well as perception of his music. It has greatly contributed toward making him the enigmatic and awesome figure he remains in music history. But if this concept may have made him appear old-fashioned to his contemporaries, it surely is one of the most forward-looking components of his strange physiognomy as a composer, for it points directly to certain ideas that have come to the fore only in very recent times. It may well be that it is mainly our affinity for the structural aspect of his music which enables us to understand and appreciate Ockeghem better than any generation before ours.

The Factor of Emotional Expression

R<small>EPEATEDLY</small> on these pages we have touched upon expressive qualities which we thought we found in Ockeghem's music. In fact it was the discovery of such qualities which made us feel close and sympathetic to this composer, after we had been enlightened in our first investigation of his music about those coldly intellectual aspects which so many historians had pointed out to his discredit. The admiration which we eventually developed for the Flemish master was to a far greater extent based on the emotional response which his music elicited than on his mastery of counterpoint, which would amount to little if the musical configuration that it produced were of merely technical interest.

From an historical viewpoint one might raise the question whether Ockeghem, or for that matter any composer of the period, intended his music to be expressive, or whether we are here reading something into the music which actually is not in it. We must admit that the subject of expression in music, which has become the cause of interminable speculation in modern times, never seemed to occupy the minds of mediaeval writers on music. Should we conclude therefrom that the music of those days was not expressive, or that its expressive qualities were taken for granted, so that there was no need for discussing them?

The answer is a little more complex than it may seem. The ancient writers wish a work of music to be "pleasant," "pleasing," "agreeable," and the like, and they expect the composer to strive for such results. Their discussions of compositional practices and the rules which they derive from their observations are meant to aid the composer in his task. However, nearly always this advice is limited to very elementary items. Even so advanced a writer as Tinctoris, who goes into considerable detail, devotes most of his labor to the analysis of materials—tones, intervals, rhythm, measurement, proportions—and in his technical instruction hardly penetrates the matter beyond explaining what intervals may be used on what conditions in order to satisfy his definitions of correct procedure. We never hear from him why he would consider one melody more beautiful than another, or how larger forms—or any musical forms, for that matter —should be constructed, and so forth. In fact, so obvious, powerful, and ubiquitous a structural vehicle as imitation— on which some more a little later—is never even mentioned.

The teachings of the theorists are indeed so elementary that hardly anybody who was able to read and to write could have failed to put together "correct" music. But it is doubtful that all successful exercises of that kind would have earned the praise of the learned critics for being "pleasing" and "agreeable." Obviously there was a wide margin between conformity with the rules and artistic excellence, and it is probably the latter which was identified with the modest label of pleasantness. But theorists did not venture into that marginal area. Rather they gave the impression—and perhaps believed it themselves—that technical perfection on an elementary level was the true source of the sought-after pleasantness.

Another question is whether the aesthetic values realized by the great composers in what we called the marginal area affected the listeners in the same way as they affect us now. The very fact that nobody seemed to be aware of those values indicates that they did not. That should not imply that we believe those people to have been unreceptive to the expressive qualities of their music. However, our emotional response to music is based on the fact that we are able to associate in our imagination certain musical elements with ideas, thoughts, sentiments, sensations, and so forth. Undoubtedly most of these associations can be traced to some ever so remote analogy, of which we are perhaps not conscious at all. On an elementary level such analogies are of a crudely imitatory or descriptive nature: musical sounds can imitate, for instance, bird calls; or a downward skip of a melody may symbolize a downward motion of some kind. Such analogies were known to mediaeval musicians, and they exploited them, though rather rarely.

The extension of this symbolism to the entire sphere of human emotions is an achievement of the Renaissance. It is the very essence of operatic music, which would be inconceivable if one could not count on the listener's making constantly and immediately the necessary associations. Whether or not any music that we hear was written with this responsive mechanism in mind does not affect our mental associations. We respond to it in terms of such associations, since this is our mode of reaction, which we can not shut off at will. Thus if we are emotionally affected by some passages in Ockeghem's music and try to describe our reaction by saying that such a passage is melancholy, or tender, or sombre, or jubilant, it matters little whether his contemporaries reacted similarly and would have used similar terms to describe their experience. Obviously the music is potentially expressive of such sentiments, and our reaction brings them out. It is this ability of evoking not only intellectual interest, but also immediate emotional reactions under completely changed social and psychological circumstances, which proves that Ockeghem's music is still alive.

The "Artifices"

THE intellectual interest, of course, emanates from the contrapuntal manipulations which, as we have seen, were the cause of Ockeghem's one-sided fame. Reading the various and generally brief references to Ockeghem in historical accounts, we get the impression that in his polyphonic writing he used the device of "imitation" permanently and exclusively. The German musicologist Riemann calls him *"der für seine Zeit massgebende Altmeister des durchimitierenden a capella Stils"* ("the dean, who for his period set the standards, of the a capella style of continuous imitation").

"Imitation," as a technical term of counterpoint, means that in a setting of several voices one of them begins alone with a melodic motive which is then repeated, or "imitated," a little later by the second, and possibly again a little later, by the third and fourth voices, while the preceding voices continue their melodic development independently. The consecutive entrances of the motive usually occur on different pitch levels. If the imitation extends beyond the opening motive, that is, if the subsequent voices continually repeat everything that the first voice has been doing, we call such a piece a "canon." It is interesting that a successful canon is

considered a particularly perfect demonstration of contrapuntal artistry, although the very idea of polyphony involves
a maximum of mutual independence among the voices.
Ostensibly, if all voices are doing the same thing, such independence can only be nullified. The point is that the com-
pulsion of continuous imitation makes it difficult for the
leading voice to proceed with freedom, elegance, expression,
and vitality, while trying to remain contrapuntally correct
in relation to the imitating voices. The challenge thus presented makes the canon a prize specimen of musical
ingenuity.

Now the truth of the matter is that Ockeghem has used
these devices very rarely in his masses—in fact, much less
consistently and with much less pedantry than some of his
younger contemporaries. The voices in his polyphonic settings are related to each other in terms of imitation, but
generally in more subtle ways than the procedure of consecutive entrances of the same material which we have described. Since the melodic material of Ockeghem's voices
is homogeneous throughout, as it is invented with reference
to the cantus firmus, there are many correspondences between the voices given from the outset. The free and non-
committal contrapuntal technique of the composer now
reveals such correspondences by stressing them through brief
literal imitations, now again conceals them by slightly mod-
ifying the rhythmic and melodic shapes of the corresponding
elements. The result is a lively and unpredictable interplay
of melodic lines, which imparts to the musical substance a
high degree of plasticity. While at the hands of minor composers of motets imitation frequently becomes a matter of
routine, a mechanical device by which a sagging musical
process can be helped along somehow, the many little in-
stances of local imitation in Ockeghem's polyphonic network
are always dictated by an ever alert inventiveness that con-
centrates upon the momentary situation.

There is only one work on a large scale by Ockeghem which is entirely based upon canonic imitation. It is the *Missa Prolationum*. The plan of this formidable composition suggests that the composer wanted to demonstrate explicitly that concept of simultaneity which we described as particularly close to the Gothic mind. The title of the mass indicates the procedure of composition. The term "prolatio" here does not designate the fastest level of the mensuration scheme, but rather suggests the idea of proportion. (The Middle Ages were no better than our own time in using technical terms loosely.) All sections of this mass are canons, many of them double canons in which two pairs of voices carry out two canons of two voices each at the same time. The majority of these canons are technically known as "mensuration canons." They differ from the simple canon in that both voices start together, instead of one after the other, but one of them presents the material of the other in a different speed, which is related to the speed of the companion voice in terms of a certain ratio. Naturally the faster of the two will cover the material in shorter time than the other voice. It then continues with new melodic developments which usually are not subject to imitation, or from a certain point on the composition will continue as a straight canon, without time differences. Various ratios are used for the divers sections of the work.

The difficult assignment is executed with remarkable elegance, and nowhere has the listener the impression that the composer was working under duress, as it were. For the real touchstone of canonic work of any kind is, of course, whether a piece written with so many conditions set up in advance sounds artistically alive and spontaneous. Any competent craftsman can put together a complicated canon and achieve correct results if he obeys the rules valid in the chosen contrapuntal style. But lesser luminaries will bog down in inventiveness, stifled by the technical obstacles of the project.

"Clefless" Compositions

ANOTHER large work that offers testimony of our composer's virtuosity in dealing with challenging difficulties is the *Missa cujusvis toni*—"Mass in Any Mode." Here the problem is not one of coordinating various preordained strains of melodies, but of calculating pitch relationships and interval combinations. The composition is written without clefs. In their place we find special symbols that look somewhat like question marks. Clefs are signs which instruct us how to read the notes on the lines of the music staff. Originally the clefs point out the place of a definite note. Thus our treble clef is also called a G-clef, for if correctly drawn, the end of its curlicue will stop exactly on the second line from bottom of our staff, and consequently we read the note which straddles that line as G. Our bass clef is an F-clef, for its two little dots stand on either side of the line whose note we read as F below middle-C. In ancient music, clefs were mainly used to indicate the line of middle-C, and while our clefs are always in the same position, the ancient C-clefs could be located on any line of the staff. The clef changed its place according to the range within which the musical phrase would move about, and the line for the clef was so chosen that the notes would as far as possible stay within the staff. The ancients preferred taking the trouble of changing the point of reference when they read the music, to having notes high above or way below the staff, presumably again to save paper. We prefer to have our clefs stationary and to read many notes with several extra lines outside of the staff. At any rate, a clef opens the way for the correct reading of the notes, whence it receives its name from the French word for "key."

70

A clefless composition like the *Missa cujusvis toni* can not be read off-hand. Proper clefs have to be chosen, one for each of the four voices. In this particular case several combinations of clefs will produce correct results, and it was for the singers, or their leader, to figure out which combination was most suitable for their voice group. If Ockeghem could expect the performers to solve the riddle, we can not have respect enough for their superior knowledge of music theory. Far less intricate problems would probably stump any singer of our day. Modern composers are far from tempted to tease their presumptive performers with riddles of any kind. They try to make their intentions as plain as possible, and if the results reasonably approximate their expectations, they are only too happy. Our respect for those singers is surpassed only by our admiration for the composer. To contrive a complex contrapuntal work whose voices can be sung in various combinations of pitch levels without obtaining the result of a meaningless caterwauling requires consummate skill bordering on the miraculous.

Another slighter composition of Ockeghem's which follows the same principle is a three-voice canon. It too is written without clefs, but here several key signatures are offered as cues for the selection of suitable pitch levels. It does not seem that this piece was destined to be used for ecclesiastical purposes. It may have been an exercise for demonstration, or such like. This composition has been frequently quoted in musical literature and certainly has contributed to Ockeghem's reputation as a "pure cerebralist." It is usually called a "fugue," but although this term was occasionally used in those days, the musical form from which the now customary definition of a fugue was derived later, especially in Bach's time, did not yet exist in the fifteenth century. Thus Kiesewetter's statement that Ockeghem's music abounds in "canons and fugues of the most manifold descriptions" is evidently misleading.

The Famous "Twittering"

T HE work which apparently preoccupied the imagination of early and late commentators on Ockeghem most permanently is the famous "twittering" in thirty-six voices. As a technical feat it is much less impressive than any of the compositions discussed so far. On account of the limited range of the human voice the parts have to move in a highly congested area and are constantly stepping on each other's toes, as it were, because most of the imitations have to start on the same pitch level, which entails a great deal of duplication of tones. Furthermore, since the stylistic conventions of the period severely restricted the use of dissonances, the consonant combinations must prevail. These, however, consist for practical purposes of three different tones only, which again means that many of the voices have to sing the same tones. (Even if the composer could have used all twelve tones of our scale freely, as we are now able to do, in a total twelve-tone chord, every tone of the twelve would still have had to be sung by at least three voices, when all thirty-six were operating together.) Thus it is inevitable that the monstrous canon lacks variety of harmonic color as well as interest and clarity of design. We are inclined to think that the composer did not attach too much importance to this exercise. To identify forever a creator of great and beautiful music with a little, and none too successful, stunt only because there is a touch of the sensational about it, takes a sort of Hollywoodian press agent's mentality which it is a little surprising to encounter in those distant days.

Subtleties of Harmonic Color

A VERY fine sense for distinctive harmonic colors is a characteristic feature of Ockeghem's personal style, quite
noticeable especially if we compare several of his masses
with each other. Nearly every one has an unmistakable flavor emanating from the combinations of chords prevailing
in it. This is a truly progressive aspect of Ockeghem's genius,
for it anticipates an awareness of harmonic values which
became a commonly shared ingredient of musical conception
only with Monteverdi, a hundred years after Ockeghem.

The *Missa Caput*, one of Ockeghem's outstanding masterworks, shows particular boldness and originality in the establishment of its basic color. There can be no doubt that
the composer was quite conscious of what he wanted to
accomplish and went about it with deliberate planning. In
the first place he put the cantus firmus into the lowest voice,
which is a very unusual arrangement, challenging our curi-
osity as to why this was done. The cantus has such a worldly
lilt that earlier commentators surmised it to be a secular
song, although no one was able to trace its origin. Only recently the sharp-eyed musicologist Manfred Bukofzer identified it as a fragment of a Gregorian melody, which was
used very rarely in the liturgical ceremony of the Washing
of Feet on Maundy Thursday. This cantus revolves around
G, with D being the tone of secondary emphasis. However,
B-natural stands out a great deal too, since the first two
phrases of the tune begin with this tone. In the conventional
style of the period it would have been normal to place the
cantus in the tenor and construct the other voices in such a
way that the G-mode would dominate the whole structure.

73

(Ockeghem's predecessor, Dufay, had done so in his mass on the same cantus firmus.)

But Ockeghem makes the D-mode the governing frame of reference and lets the music harmonically swing back and forth between G and D. This procedure makes the B, which lies halfway between G and D, a sort of pivot around which the harmonic processes revolve each time when the cantus furnishes the B. Now the B is a very precarious tone to have used as the fundamental of a chord in those days, since the regular three-voiced chord established upon B will read B-D-F. It includes between its highest and lowest tones the interval of a diminished fifth, which because of its dissonant implications was regarded by the theorists with utmost suspicion. The conventions of the time allowed the composer, and the singer, to correct situations in which the alarming combination occurred by either lowering the B-natural to B-flat, or, more rarely, by raising the F to F sharp.

Close examination of the *Missa Caput* reveals that in the majority of cases—and there are indeed so many diminished fifths in it, on account of the ever recurring long B's in the bass, that one might call them the *leitmotiv*, or the leading motive, of the mass—such corrections would not remedy the irregularity, for these corrections would create equally objectionable diminished fifths at a different place in the context. There is additional evidence supporting the assumption that Ockeghem was intent upon using those intervals, in the face of the stern injunctions of every theorist past and present. In fact it is this swinging back and forth between the somewhat gloomy D-chords and the serene G-chords through the intermediate station of those hollow and mournful harmonies established on B which gives this composition a unique, haunting flavor strangely intermingling raucous melancholy, subdued radiance, and shadowy darkness.

In the *Missa Serviteur* it is again a characteristic feature of the cantus firmus which is exploited to impart to the whole work a characteristic harmonic color. Here the first phrase of the cantus moves downward from C to D, and by letting the contrapuntal voices run through the same configurations each time this phrase appears, the composer throws into relief the rather unusual change in a very short span of modal reference from C to D. The general tone of the *Missa Serviteur* is sombre and solemn. Some scholars doubt that Ockeghem was the author of this mass and are inclined to think that it should be ascribed to a contemporary named Faugues. We are in no way equipped to decide a question of that kind. However, if internal evidence should count at all, it strongly speaks in favor of Ockeghem's authorship, as the style of the work shows many of the typical traits of our composer.

The harmonic world of Ockeghem's masses written in the F-modality is of a distinctly different character. Their harmonic color gives them a prevailingly serene and friendly atmosphere. There is a *Missa Quinti Toni* in three voices, without a set cantus firmus. (According to the ancient nomenclature the F-mode was known as the fifth in the table of the modes, *quintus tonus.*) The "Et incarnatus est" in the Credo of this mass has a particularly mystical quality, and at the words "Et ascendit in coelum" the two voices that are singing that part of the text are set at a most unusually wide distance from each other, very suggestive of the infinite elevation of the heavenly spheres over the darkening depth of the earth from which Christ had risen. A triumphant note is unmistakable in "Et iterum venturus est," and the sudden drop of the voice lines an octave down from "vivos" to "mortuos" is, to our knowledge, the first illustration in history of the contrast of the "quick and the dead," an illustration that later became standard procedure in many masses. In these discreet and original attempts at using mus-

ical means to symbolize important turns of the text Ockeghem again appears quite progressive.

Another particularly elegant and lovely "missa quinti
toni" is the *Missa Ma Maitresse,* in which Ockeghem uses
the complicated and lively tune of his own delightful chanson "Ma Maitresse" as cantus firmus. Unfortunately this
mass is not extant in complete form. Other masses on secular cantus firmi are titled *De plus en plus, Au travail je suis,
Fort seulement,* and *L'homme armé.* The tune last named
was one of the most popular with religious composers and
has been used over and over again into Palestrina's time.
Apparently its simple, angular phrases and their sequence
and mutual relationship recommended it as a basic pattern
for the kind of polyphonic design which was desired. Apart
from the *Missa Caput,* there is only one other mass by
Ockeghem that has a Gregorian cantus firmus, the *Ecce
Ancilla Domini.*

One of Ockeghem's "missae sine nomine," has the curious
title *Missa Mi-Mi,* which refers to the fact that the bass part
in each movement begins with the melodic progression E-A.
In the ancient nomenclature the tone was called Mi (the
third in the sequence Do-Re-Mi-Fa-Sol-La). This coincides
with the usage still prevailing in Romance languages, in
which our C corresponds to the ancient Do. However, the
mediaevalists did not think in terms of a unified system of
octaves as we do, but employed as a frame of reference three
"hexachords," that is, scales of six tones each beginning on
our C, F, and G respectively. In each of these the first tone
was called Do. Consequently our A is not only the last
tone of the hexachord of C, as which it is called La, but it
is also identical with the third tone of the hexachord on F,
and if so identified, it becomes Mi. Hence what we simply
call E-A, is in terms of that ancient system Mi-Mi—which is
another footnote to the enigmatic ways of the mediaeval
mind.

It seems that Ockeghem was the first composer who wrote a complete setting for the *Requiem* mass. The text deviates somewhat from the now customary selection, since liturgical forms of the service for the dead at that time were not yet definitely codified.

Manuscripts and Editions

M ANY manuscripts of Ockeghem's music are located in Rome. It is hard to say whether this indicates that his religious works were performed there in ecclesiastical services. In view of the fact that many Flemish and Burgundian composers traveled to Italy and some of them found employment there for extended periods of time, it is likely that Ockeghem's works were well known in the south. Some copies were found in the musicologists' treasure chest of the so-called Codices of Trent. The small town of Trent lies in that part of southern Tyrol which Austria had to cede to Italy after World War I. It is best known as the seat of the interminable Council of Trent which, in the face of the Protestant rebellion, deliberated for many years around the middle of the sixteenth century as to the ways in which the Roman Church could protect itself from further disintegration. It is well known that the question of ecclesiastical music came up for discussion too, which gave origin to the Palestrina legend. One could imagine that the Codices, which contain mainly music of the fifteenth century, served the musical experts of the Council as a sort of reference library.

While Trent still belonged to Austria, seven volumes of music, containing 1,585 compositions, were discovered in the attic of the episcopal palace of Trent. The bundle was bought by the Imperial Library of Vienna, and part of the material was published in modern critical editions by the Institute of Music History at the University of Vienna in its magnificent collection of ancient music, called *Denkmaeler der Tonkunst in Oesterreich* ("Monuments of the Tonal Art in Austria"). Some of Ockeghem's masses came for the first time to light in volume 38 of the Monuments, in 1912.

Later a young musicologist of Yugoslavian origin, of the name of Dragan Plamenac, who studied at the University of Vienna, became interested in Ockeghem, to whose motets he devoted his doctor's dissertation. Plamenac remained faithful to his preoccupation and began to prepare a critical edition of the master's complete works. The first volume of that edition appeared in 1927 in Germany as part of a collection called *Publikationen Älterer Musik* ("Publications of Rather Ancient Music"). It contains eight masses. Political conditions in Germany interrupted Mr. Plamenac's work, but he was able to bring the material which he had collected to the United States of America, where he kept working on his Ockeghem edition. The second volume was published in this country with the aid of the American Musicological Society in 1947, adding seven more masses to the complete work. It is expected that the third and final volume, containing the motets, canons, and secular compositions by Ockeghem, will be offered to the public in due course.

Various details of these editions are a matter of debate among musicologists. If there is more than one copy of a work in existence, these copies frequently show different readings of some passages, and the reasons for which one scholar preferred a certain version may not always be shared by his colleagues. Some of the copies may have been made by careless scribes, and whether any of the copies which have come down to us were seen and proofread by the composer is more than doubtful. Furthermore the tricky details of mensural notation are oftentimes very hard to decipher and may allow of more than one interpretation. Among scholars there is a widespread tendency to become alarmed by results of their readings which seem to indicate bold and unconventional procedure on the part of the composers. They are apt to suspect at such places graphical errors which they try to "correct" so that the passage will conform to what the particular musicologist believes to be the commonly accepted stylistic habit of the period. Again others seem to be so unconcerned with the musical aspects of what appears to them as a correct reading of their sources that they let pass some rather unlikely details, which in turn earns them severe censure from some of their colleagues.

The modern musician who for various reasons is interested in the creative efforts of bygone ages is deeply grateful to the historians for making the ancient music available to him in readable shape. At the same time he declares himself totally incompetent so far as involving himself in the controversies which affect the scientific accuracy of the musicologists' research is concerned. It seems unfair to him to take sides in the sometimes acrimonious arguments of his learned friends, none of whom he would like to consider a fumbling ignoramus. Granting that many a passage may allow different interpretations to even the most conscientious and responsible scholar, the modern musician will always be inclined to prefer the reading which suggests the highest degree of musical interest, as it most clearly reveals the genius of the composer, in whose favor his present-day colleague is quite naturally biased. To him the material which the historians put at his disposal is a most welcome point of departure for a different type of study which is mainly concerned with the appreciation and evaluation of the artistic merits of ancient music. He wishes this music to speak to him directly, and he derives profound satisfaction from the discovery that many of the ideas, impulses, principles which animate his own work were active in the creation of music at all times, though they manifested themselves through different media in many fascinating ways conditioned by the state of mind, material, and technique of another age.

The Great Teacher

IT IS entirely possible that the availability of Ockeghem's works in our time will bring some of his music to life, as soon as performers, mainly choral conductors, feel tempted to produce it in spite of its unusual difficulties, and the impression that such performances will undoubtedly create may influence in some way the musical thinking of present-day composers. The modern composer will be especially attracted to Ockeghem by the master's unusual and imaginative treatment of dissonance, by his boundless freedom in rhythmic and metric matters, and by his capacity for spinning forth tirelessly vibrating melodic lines over extraordinary spans. Present-day composers who practice the twelve-tone technique will be interested in the ways in which Ockeghem used his "basic patterns," the cantus firmi, to create structural unity in large musical areas. One of the most inspiring elements should be observation of the sovereignty with which Ockeghem mustered his resources, switching from the forceful discipline of elaborate contrapuntal technique to unrestricted interplay of melodic forces, never committing himself to any rigid method.

Of course such influence, which is based on being inspired by a great example in general ways rather than on learning practical procedure, would be of a totally different nature from the direct influence that Ockeghem exerted upon his own and the following generation, when composers still wrote in the same idiom as he did and expressed themselves through the same media. This influence must have been rather extraordinary, for he is constantly described as a teacher of uncommon qualities. Once in a while we get the impression that historians have overemphasized this aspect of his personality, as if they felt guilty for not having much good to say about him otherwise and wanted to compensate for this by praising his pedagogical excellence. For instance, Grove's Dictionary says that "these masses exhibit Ockeghem as a great teacher rather than a great church composer" and quotes the inevitable Kiesewetter to the effect that "as a teacher Ockeghem stands alone in the whole history of music." It is hard to see how one can tell from anybody's compositions that he was a teacher rather than a composer, since the only way of evaluating a teacher is to find out whether he had any students who amounted to something, and what accomplishments of their own they had learned from him. Kiesewetter's statement must be qualified as an untenable exaggeration, even without investigation of the case.

The composers consistently listed as pupils of Ockeghem are Josquin de Prés, Pierre de la Rue, Brumel, and Compère. There must have been many others, but their names would mean even less to us than those mentioned here, with the exception of Josquin de Prés, who has remained the only pre-Palestrinian composer of permanent fame. All of these authors seem to have inherited from their master his virtuosity in dealing with intricate contrapuntal problems. In fact they appear to have dedicated themselves to the manufacture of the famous "artifices" to a much larger extent than Ockeghem, who had to take the blame of being an intellectualist. What distinguishes those composers from Ockeghem is mainly that much of his ruggedness and unpredictability is missing in their music. Their work shows more elegance, smoothness, and poise, which is indicative of the trend announced by Tinctoris and others.

In this respect those younger composers may have taken a leaf out of the book of Ockeghem's great Dutch contemporary, Jacob Obrecht. In view of the course that the evolution of music took it is perhaps justified to call Obrecht more progressive than Ockeghem, as some scholars do. His music, generally well-poised and sedate, has great dignity, but it certainly is much less exciting than Ockeghem's, and therefore to us does not sound particularly progressive. The younger composers evolved more typical procedures of treating dissonances than those applied by Ockeghem, thus preparing the way for the standardization of the Palestrina age, and the technique of imitation which we have discussed earlier becomes highly regularized. While the chief merit of the lesser composers of the period mainly consists in working out a generally acceptable and easily comprehensible style of polyphonic writing, Josquin de Prés, a genius of first magnitude, made up for the softening of edges through superior invention and profound sentiment. He also introduced new harmonic ideas to which he may well have been inspired by the keen sensitivity for harmonic shadings of his master. These innovations foreshadowed the concept of modulation which came into its own as soon as the ancient modal idiom gave way to the modern language of tonality.

The Distant Friend

Ockeghem's fame as a composer of live music has not survived this momentous change that affected the very foundations of musical concepts. Palestrina is the only one of the pre-Baroque composers who has exerted direct influence on the development of Western music to this day. It is not unlikely that, as some historians indicate, Ockeghem at the end of his life was an isolated figure, since the trend of the period was rapidly moving away from the ideals that animated his creative work. Glareanus, who wrote his *Dode-kachordon* only sixty years after Ockeghem's death—which approximately corresponds to our distance from Brahms and Tschaikowsky—already speaks of him as of an interesting, but not too clearly defined, figure of the past—a fact which should make us think twice before we praise or condemn our own age for its supposedly breathtaking speed of living. After that Ockeghem's name was remembered only in that curiously warped connotation which we have discussed on the early pages of this paper. The time has come to bring him out of the shadows which have engulfed his memory for several hundred years.

While we now can at least and at last read his music, and in the course of time should be able to enjoy hearing some of it, we do not know anything about the man who wrote it, except what transpires from the meager information on his life and what we may try to infer from his musical work. Was he a happy man? How did he spend his days and nights? Was he melancholy, solitary, gay, gregarious? Did he have a family? What was his attitude toward women? There is little hope that any new intelligence on any one of these points will ever come to light.

One might say that Ockeghem must have been possessed of some social graces, of natural psychological skill in dealing with his fellow men, and a good measure of stability of character, or else he would not have been able to secure for himself at a relatively early age such a socially significant position as that of a treasurer of St. Martin in Tours and to hold on to it for thirty-five years during a period of unrest and changing political administrations. On the other hand, his music reveals a man who was by no means a conformist, who dared to venture into territories off the beaten track according to his own lights, a man whose interior being was shaken by sudden, unpredictable impulses, and who had an unusual sensitivity for fine, delicate shadings of sentiment which he did not hesitate to express in rather unconventional ways. The unconventional, non-conformist traits in Ockeghem's nature seem to be indicative of a mysticism that, as a late, last flowering of the Gothic mentality, must have appeared anachronistic in an atmosphere of growing rationality. At the same time these traits were prophetic of things to come in a much later age. Yet Ockeghem must have been communicative, eloquent, and convincing in his utterance, or else he would not have attracted so many students and been generally recognized as a pedagogical genius.

We can not hope to reconstruct Ockeghem's personality from the unrelated fragments of observation which we try to assemble, as an object of great magnitude moves rapidly through the beam of our feeble searchlight at a distance of five hundred years. The only thing which we discern with increasing clarity is the gentle and exciting shimmer that reflects from the master's music as we turn our loving gaze on its amazing features.

Los Angeles, California
May 25, 1952

Bibliography

I. *Music*

A.1. Editions of Ockeghem's masses:

JOHANNES OCKEGHEM, *Saemtliche Werke,* vol. i, ed. Dragan Plamenac, in: *Publikationen aelterer Musik,* vol. i, ii, 1927.

JOHANNES OCKEGHEM, *Completed Works,* vol. ii, ed. Dragan Plamenac, New York, 1947.

Denkmaeler der Tonkunst in Oesterreich, XIX, vol. 38, Wien, 1912.

A.2. Fragments, excerpts, etc. of Ockeghem's music, in:

A. W. AMBROS (see below).

M. BUKOFZER (see below).

A. T. DAVISON and W. APEL, *Historical Anthology of Music,* Cambridge (Mass.), 1946.

O. GOMBOSI (see below).

Oxford History of Music (see below).

A. SCHERING, *Geschichte der Musik in Beispielen,* Leipzig, 1931.

B. Recordings:

JOHANNES OCKEGHEM, *Ma maitresse* (three-part chanson, in French), in: *Anthologie sonore,* vol. i.   AS-3

JOHANNES OCKEGHEM, *Missa L'homme armé* (Credo).   G-W 1513

II. *Reading Material*

A. About Johannes Ockeghem directly:

a) Books

MARIE BOBILLIER (pseud.: Michel Brenet), *Jean de Ockeghem,* in: *Mémoires de la societé de l'histoire de Paris et de l'Isle-de-France,* vol. xx, 1893.

DE BUBURE, *Jean de Ockeghem,* in: *Annales du cercle archéologique de Trémonde,* 1868.

DE MARCY, *Jean Ockeghem,* 1895.

D. PLAMENAC, *Johannes Ockeghem als Motetten- und Chansonskomponist,* Wien, 1925.

b) Articles

R. G. HARRIS, "An Analysis of the Design of the 'Caput' Masses by Dufay and Ockeghem in Their Metric and Rhythmic Aspects," in: *Hamline Studies in Musicology*, ed. E. Krenek, vol. i, St. Paul (Minn.), 1945.

E. KRENEK, "A Discussion of the Treatment of Dissonances in Ockeghem's Masses as Compared with the Contrapuntal Theory of Johannes Tinctoris," in: *Hamline Studies . . .* (see above), vol. ii, 1947.

J. S. LEVITAN, "Ockeghem's Clefless Compositions," in: *Musical Quarterly*, vol. xiii, no. 4, Oct. 1937.

V. SEAY, "A Contribution to the Problem of Mode in Mediaeval Music," in: *Hamline Studies . . .* (see above), vol. i, 1945.

B. General references:

A. W. AMBROS, *Geschichte der Musik*, vol. iii, Leipzig, 1862-1882.

W. APEL, *Harvard Dictionary of Music*, Cambridge (Mass.), 1944.

W. APEL, *The Notation of Polyphonic Music, 900-1600*, Cambridge (Mass.), 1942.

M. BUKOFZER, *Studies in Medieval and Renaissance Music*, New York, 1950.

H. COUSSEMAKER, *Scriptorum de musica medii aevi . . .* , 1864.

H. GLAREANUS, *Dodekachordon*, Basel, 1547.

O. GOMBOSI, *Jacob Obrecht*, Leipzig, 1925.

C. GRAY, *The History of Music*, London, 1928.

GROVE'S *Dictionary of Music and Musicians*, 1904-1910.

P. H. LANG, *Music in Western Civilization*, New York, 1941.

Oxford History of Music, vols. i, ii, Oxford, 1901-1905.

G. REESE, *Music in the Middle Ages*, New York, 1940.

H. RIEMANN, *Musiklexikon* (11. Auflage), Berlin, 1929.

J. TINCTORIS, *Liber de arte contrapuncti*, 1477, in: Coussemaker, *Scriptorum . . .* (see above).